CW01021193

RAFAEL MOSCATEL

The Bastard of Beverly Hills

JIA PUBLISHING

First published by JIA Publishing Group 2023

Visit www.jiapublishing.com to read more about all our books and to buy them. You will also find features, author interviews, and news of any author events, and you can sign up for e-newsletters so that you're always first to hear about our new releases.

Library of Congress Control Number: 2023904249

First edition

ISBN: 979-8-9879061-6-3

Editing by Abby Jane Moscatel

This book was professionally typeset on Reedsy.
Find out more at reedsy.com

For Albert

Better is open rebuke than hidden love.

— Proverbs 27:5

Contents

Preface

I grew up thinking the old days were like silent movies, shot in black and white and mostly forgotten.

Picturing them through a bleak, monochrome lens helped me brush aside my past much the same way, witlessly discarding any faded scenes that, in color, may have revealed more than I wanted.

Then well into adulthood, a voice behind me yelled, "Cut!"

I turned back and discovered I'd been adopted. *Lied to my whole life.*

In an instant, all I'd come to know of myself seemed to vanish. No past, present, or future remained to which I belonged. A fuse had blown, and the universe became a darkroom.

When I awoke, my yesterdays in Los Angeles slowly resurfaced, like a dusty film reel dropped from a staircase, unspooling down each step—its tiny, perforated frames emblazoned with famous faces in whose company the truth was concealed.

I endeavored to develop the negatives, hoping a reliable image might arise from the emulsion. But how do you arrange a carousel of grey, disjointed memories hidden for over thirty years?

That answer materialized one evening in the advice of an angelic widow I'd once worked beside in a bookshop. With so many chapters of her life spent perusing the shelves, she'd become a hunchback, her spine nearly broken.

Upon hearing my dilemma, she gently took my hand as if to read it.

"I know of only seven stories in this world," she said, tracing a line in my palm. "Just seven stories even the most ambitious writer could hope to reconstrue—a tragedy, a comedy, the journey, a quest, the rags-to-riches fable, a rebirth, and the tale of a monster."

Then, staring into my hungry eyes, she leaned in and whispered, "Which one is yours?"

Suddenly, I knew.

Monsters

That hideous beast. It murdered my best friend one New Year's Eve, leaving his bruised, punctured corpse to rot all week on the floor of a Malibu drug den. He died steps from the same sandy beach where, as blood brothers with matching bowl cuts and our third-grade imaginations, we'd once frolicked morning to night, burying treasures at the foot of a rocky cove. The aroma of embers crackling in a nearby bonfire signaled it was time for supper.

Now I'm haunted by a different scent. A stench, really. One that lingered like a fume well after Scotty's interment. It was a day of reckoning, an unearthly event that, ever since, has served as a line of demarcation between the rebellious child I was and the man I'd have to become.

His funeral was the day I quit smoking. I marked the date with a sharpie across the cellophane on my last pack. Each year, around the time of his death, I pull it out, recalling battles we fought against that monster as troubled kids. The smell of the stale tobacco inside still reminds me of our friendship and the precise moment of our fates' divergence.

My son was just an infant when Scotty passed. As I chain-smoked on the balcony, waiting for my wife, Abby, I could hear the boy wheezing. I never lit up in our apartment, but the carbon monoxide often seeped into the nursery like a ghost.

The sitter arrived. I put out my cigarette in a dirty tin ashtray on the ledge.

"We should go," I muttered to Abby, forgetting to lock the sliding glass door behind me.

"Is this okay?" she asked softly, adjusting the neckline of her black collared dress.

I nodded but didn't much care.

A genteel, midwest girl, Abby usually knew the right look for any occasion. I'd taken her suggestion and worn the skinny tie and charcoal suit that hadn't been out of the dry-cleaning plastic since our wedding. We were exhausted like all new parents. The crow's feet around my blue eyes were evidence of sleepless nights and a spate of recent arguments.

As we rode an elevator to the garage, she held back her auburn hair so I could refasten the clasp on the pendant I'd gifted her when we started dating. It always seemed to come loose.

We drove to the cemetery without saying a word.

She parked her silver Mazda behind a line of fancy cars as I checked my voicemail. Eleanor, my mother, had left instructions on where to find her and Dad once we'd arrived. I was the only one of her children there—my two older sisters unwilling to travel.

Paparazzi were camped outside the chapel that brisk morning. As I walked past, one mumbled to another, "I think it's Ed Norton."

"Nah, too short," the other quipped.

I winced at the comparison, coughing as we ascended the front stoop, proceeding through the white Tuscan columns at the entrance and down the sanctuary's middle aisle. A sunbeam pierced the stained glass and fell upon my friend's closed casket. It froze me in my tracks, a morbid centerpiece radiating with lifelessness. I felt the gravity of the coffin bearing down on the bier as if, at any moment, it might collapse under its own weight and tumble down the altar.

Somebody nudged me, and I kept moving.

I sat a few rows back with my father, Ray, and opened the program. The mortuary's template had been edited with an outdated photo of Scotty looking uncomfortable in a polyester button-down. On the next page was the twenty-third Psalm. I read the first few lines.

The LORD is my shepherd; I shall not want.
He maketh me to lie down in green pastures.
He leadeth me beside the still waters.
He restoreth my soul.

I folded the pamphlet and tucked it into a breast pocket.

Glancing to my side, I noticed the distinct striped suspenders of Larry King, a talk show host and friend of the grieving Sterling family. His arms and legs were crossed as he inspected me through his horn-rimmed glasses.

"How-ya-doin'?" he asked in a thick Brooklyn accent, greeting me warmly and extending a clammy handshake.

I'd met the interviewer once before, while home from college one summer and clerking at a bookstore. He'd popped in to see if we were carrying his latest title. I didn't bother to bring that up, and he wouldn't have recognized me anyhow.

But as surreal as it felt sitting next to him at the funeral that day, it couldn't compare to the disturbing sequence of events about to unfold as we laid my dear friend to rest.

* * *

Piecing together my scattered thoughts and feelings around Scotty's death had taken a back seat to relationships, children, and a career. Those are all gifts he wasn't afforded. And you can probably find plenty of folks who either loathed or loved the guy but will never find anyone who understood his anguish the way I did. Our bond was forged in the striking similarities of our upbringing—given up by reckless mothers and placed with eccentric families living right across the street from one another. Through the years, my ship would navigate rough seas while Scotty's would sink into an abyss. His lot became a pit of despair from which, like the Hebrew, Joseph, he couldn't climb out.

The last time I'd seen him was three months before his funeral, outside my parents' house on Beverly Drive, the morning of my son's bris. The street was quiet except for the passing hum of motorists and wild parrots squawking in the swaying palm trees.

He'd borrowed my lighter, and we stood shoulder to shoulder on the uneven sidewalk, catching up on better times. His hair had been buzzed, and his pupils were dilated. He mentioned he'd been working out, but his clothes were too big for his frame.

"Congrats, Bucky," he said in a raspy voice, his hands shaking as he wiped the drip from his nose.

Scotty must have been the only person who still called me by that handle.

He stared down past Sunset Boulevard at his parents' walled mansion on the corner. I hadn't seen him in a while but sensed his need to be closer and confide. That fork in the road where we'd separated was miles behind us. He was backtracking, desperately trying to find signs pointing the way home. A home he wished looked more like mine.

"Auntie Ellie told me you found out about your adoption."

That's what everybody called my mom, *Auntie Ellie*.

I took a short drag and admitted, "Couple of years ago, but yeah."

"Cool, cool," he replied, blowing a plume toward the empty sky.

His motive surfaced as he ruminated on repressed emotions, seemingly eager to learn about his own ordeal but overwhelmed by the prospect of investigating it. Unlike me, Scotty had known he wasn't his parents' biological son from early on but was discouraged from seeking answers. Out of fear or shame, he'd avoided openly expressing any desire to know a family separate from the one that raised him. Yet, seeing how the discovery was transforming me made him reconsider.

I regret not helping him take the next step.

But now that I'm exhuming Scotty's spirit, I owe it to both of us to set the record straight about our adoptions in the manner he would have wanted and deserved. I cared for him, despite his flaws. And I know his brother, sister, and mother did so, too. But time and again, the one person whose love he needed most was never there—his father, Donald Sterling.

I'd only seen *Uncle Don*, an honorific title bestowed on him by my mother, once between my son's birth and the morning of his son's burial. He'd been shopping on Western Avenue with a paramour. His rampant infidelity wasn't news. Indeed, it formed the basis of widespread rumors and lawsuits. But it was the first time I'd seen him with my own eyes engaged in an extra-marital affair. Since he always thought of me as a boy, the old man was abashed, like the guilty child caught with his hand in a cookie jar.

He was greasy as I gazed upon him that day. It brought back memories of sleepovers and playdates at Scotty's house as if they'd just been captured on Kodachrome. Don sauntered about in his monogrammed ivory bathrobe, his dyed black hair combed back, rolling phone calls on a rotary dial. In between, he'd bark orders and criticism at his boy, like, "God damn it, close the door when you come back in this house!" and "Shut your mouth when I'm on the phone!"

Yet, in public, Don was gregarious and guarded his vulnerabilities closely. He'd grown up poor and disadvantaged in Boyle Heights and never discussed his childhood. At times, Scotty tried in vain to speak tenderly to him, but the man was iron-hearted and indifferent. People say that's the cruelest form of punishment. Well, for Scotty, it was true.

Nothing was worse than having a father who didn't want him around.

My friend and I began our lives as fragile souls. We were both abandoned, which made assimilating into the upper crust of Beverly Hills, at least subconsciously, an unnatural adaptation. And Scotty's early traumatic experiences with his dad may have saddled him with the kind of baggage not easily unpacked by a shrink. Don never handed out more than a spanking, from what I observed. But it didn't matter. The apathy he treated that boy with did more damage than a leather belt ever could.

As a father, I've tried to put myself in Don's loafers and speculate what may have gone wrong between him and Scotty, who was frequently in legal trouble. A part of me wants to believe he was demonstrating love for the boy all those times he shielded him from the long arm of the law. But he was likely more interested in protecting his reputation.

When Scotty was nineteen, Don intervened to prevent him from being charged with the attempted murder of a man he'd been fighting with over a girl. The *LA Times*, in their coverage of his son's overdose, rehashed the allegation.

> The shooting occurred at the Beverly Hills home of Donald Sterling—lawyer, commercial real estate mogul, owner of the Clippers basketball team and fundraiser for outgoing District Attorney Gil Garcetti. More than a year after the shooting, prosecutors decided not to file charges. The conclusion left police frustrated.

That outgoing district attorney was Don's friend and benefactor of his recurring political contributions. Everybody suspected that their relationship influenced why charges weren't filed. Beyond injustice to the alleged victim, though, it was a disservice to Scotty. I can't help but wonder whether things would have turned out differently if that compromised DA hadn't interfered and let him face the music.

One thing is certain—the favor didn't help Scotty in his struggle with the monster. He may have thought he'd slipped from its grip, but that salivating beast grew mightier with each passing day. It was our Leviathan. Serpent-like and demonic, its blazing eyes feasted on our insecurities, constantly tempting us to seek validation from the bottom of a flask, the tip of a syringe, the end of a joint, or the arms of a submissive lover.

I can't remember if Gil Garcetti attended Scotty's funeral. But I watched him deliver the keynote at a friend's gala a few years later. He conducted himself like an elder statesman up there on the dais, speaking glowingly about his son, Eric, newly elected to the LA City Council. It crossed my mind to confront him about my friend.

It wouldn't have been the first time.

Ten years before, I'd had too much to drink at Scotty's sister's wedding and brazenly called out the attorney for mishandling the infamous OJ Simpson trial. My unsolicited opinions, awkwardly timed moments before the bride walked down the aisle, annoyed Garcetti. He laughed off my outburst, but it must have been brought to Uncle Don's attention because he treated me a little differently from that point. It angered him, perhaps rightly, that I'd disrupted the occasion. By the time I saw his old crony speak years later at the gala, I'd matured. With a young family and a burgeoning career, I knew better.

They would both be judged, but not by me, I told myself as the rabbi opened Scotty's service.

As he spoke, I looked at the back of Don's head in the front row of the opposite aisle. He turned around to check attendance, then reclined as if it were another day at the office.

The man was unaffected, just like in business, where he'd employed a strategy that could be summed up in two words—*never sell.* Take his basketball club, the Clippers, for example. Season after season, they finished in last place. Fans never caught on that Sterling had no intention of winning. The team was little more than a financial instrument moonlighting as the mogul's toy. Don shared in NBA profits for merchandise and wrote off ticket sale losses on a separate ledger. He was even shrewder in real estate, acquiring over two hundred properties with sometimes little or no money down.

If only he'd made those wise investments in his son, I thought, sitting in the pew.

Scotty's mom, by contrast, wasn't cutthroat like her husband. She'd asked me earlier in the week to serve as a pallbearer and deliver a eulogy. At the last minute, though, Don decided to exclude me from the latter honor. He may have feared what I might say, knowing I'd seen the skeletons in his closet. Maybe he remembered my words with the DA at his daughter's wedding or when I'd caught him buying things for his mistress. Perhaps it was something else entirely. But as dismayed as I was, I'd never, in that solemn setting, trample on his family's name. I knew the right place and time would eventually come to honor Scotty.

* * *

The memory of his funeral plays back in my head like a broken record. There was sympathy for the deceased, but the event's orchestration made it ring hollow. It wasn't a funeral as much as it was a formality.

We were sitting in the third row because Don reserved the first two benches for his basketball team. Scotty's tearful girlfriend and her mother had mistakenly sat there, directly in front of me. Abby and I watched, aghast, as they were reseated toward the back of the chapel.

Invitees trickled in, a handful in wheelchairs, including an aunt who'd doted on Scotty and would leave flowers at his gravesite until her dying day. One of Don's players, a star forward, helped the woman to her seat. Then the rest of the Clippers tarried in behind him, one by one, seven feet at a time, and sat up front, blocking the view of family and friends. They were obliged to attend. But Scotty would have loved seeing them there since it's where he spent so much time—puttering around the old stadium like a lost puppy. Players and staff usually kept an eye on him in the corridors and at the concession stands before games.

His sister gave the first eulogy, and an acquaintance delivered another. After the speeches, we walked through the cemetery to where Scotty would lie forever in a mausoleum. His sister wept as she said farewell, and his mother kissed his mahogany casket.

And then all eyes turned to Don.

He stepped forward from behind his wife, already wearing his trench coat and sunglasses, as if he couldn't wait to leave. Taking a quick breath, he callously tossed a single rose onto the coffer, grimacing as he watched us slide his son into his final resting place.

* * *

Abby drove home as I smoked the last cigarette in my pack, reliving those moments of mourning with Don flinging the red rose onto Scotty's coffin. The imagery was gut-wrenching—not just Don's smugness but the ominous shadow of the beast who stalked us as kids and had wantonly claimed Scotty. The boy's spirit was engulfed in flames almost from the moment the Sterlings brought him home. Now there was nothing left to incinerate. And though I'd kept a safer distance from that monster's fire, I knew it could rise from its lair and torch me when I'd least expected it.

My son was cranky when we returned to our apartment. Abby relieved the babysitter, and I stayed behind in the kitchen. I leaned against the laminate counter, and an electric tingle rippled through my chest. Foolishly, I headed to the corner gas station for more smokes but felt another sharp pang on the walk back. This time it was excruciating.

As if I'd been struck by lightning.

I knew I'd be dead if I ever lit up again.

The warning was from Scotty, coming from somewhere in the ether. I scribbled the date on the cellophane wrapper and crumpled the pack of cigarettes with my fist.

Nicotine withdrawal ensued. I sweated through the sheets for weeks as I lay next to Abby, waking from nightmares I hadn't endured since I was a child. I kept myself up, questioning whether Scotty's life might have been saved had he connected with his blood relatives the way I originally planned.

I'd learned the secret of my adoption not long before the funeral. And it came as one hell of a surprise when I tracked down the person who made it all possible—the absolute last soul on earth you'd ever trust to watch out for a kid like me.

Riches

Behind the gates of those gilded estates in Beverly Hills lie motives and motifs found in every neighborhood—greed and charity, fear and courage, loyalty and betrayal, the most magical things and the most mundane. Mom and Dad moved into that famous little town fifty years ago but could never buy a lot there today.

Not even a tiny one.

Their 1912 Monterey Colonial is the oldest house on the block. Grainy photos of the Beverly Hills Hotel under construction show our home in the foreground, all by its lonesome in what was then a bean field. It belonged to the hotel's first owner, and the Moscatels purchased it in the seventies from the actress who played Morticia on *The Addams Family*.

The only thing that woman left on the property was the Peacock chair she memorably sat in on the television show. Mom never met the lady or watched her program but kept that chair around because she thought it nicely matched our patio's lattice. I saw it as a brittle piece of wicker furniture gathering dust, not understanding its portentous significance for years.

I always felt weird sitting in it.

Rarely did I stray from that house. Until junior high, I was either at Scotty's, teetering along the edges of a koi pond in a nearby park, or daydreaming in my bedroom as I bounced a ball off a Lakers poster. Both of my older sisters were sheltered, too. Our parents were the types to cover our eyes in theaters when movies got violent and our ears if a conversation became explicit. They didn't want us to grow up so fast that we'd forget what it was like when the only monsters in life were the ones under the bed.

Eleanor and Ray, my guardians, rarely experienced that kind of security growing up. They were first-generation immigrants living near the bottom of the food chain. In the aftermath of the first world war, Eleanor's mother, Mama Rita, and her seven siblings fled the Isle of Rhodes, a small Mediterranean island, with their few possessions. They journeyed west in search of opportunity.

My given name, Rafael, was in honor of one of them. He landed in Panama and found work repairing the canal but perished from malaria shortly afterward.

Mama Rita, an exquisite beauty and linguist, disembarked from her boat further north in Havana, where several other Sephardic Jews had settled. Cuba was a paradise that reminded her of the old country. Yet, she soon emigrated to California to wed a naturalized citizen, my grandfather, Dr. Robert. He'd made her acquaintance while visiting the island, struck up a correspondence, and seduced her with a flurry of love letters.

Aside from being a romantic and eloquent writer, the doctor was, by most appearances, a pillar of his community. Throughout his life, he fervently advocated for equal justice and human rights. My fondest childhood memories remain of the wiry, bespectacled physician delivering impassioned speeches before every meal.

Stridently enunciating as he stood at the head of the table, he'd say, "My children, my children, never forget how lucky we are—to live here, in America!"

My mother never did.

* * *

Eleanor, a feisty, ugly duckling brought up during the Great Depression, didn't complain about her humble beginnings. She wore adversity like a badge of pride. It was a defense mechanism developed at age six after being chased home by bullies hurling anti-Semitic slurs and pelting her with rocks. Determined not to play the victim, she pummeled those boys as soon as she learned to throw a right hook. Elementary school made her even tougher. And at eleven, Dr. Robert had to read her the riot act for joyriding in his sedan—though she could barely see above the dashboard. But discipline only seemed to embolden the girl.

Frustrated and short-tempered, her father turned abusive, openly worrying his daughter wouldn't amount to anything. He even sent her to live with a cousin in Seattle for a year. After she turned eighteen, however, Mom blossomed. She bleached her hair blonde, cultivated good fashion sense, and brimmed with self-confidence.

The doctor had trouble keeping up with Eleanor's modern ambition, which he chalked up to restlessness. But it wasn't the sole reason his influence over her waned. She'd discovered he was performing abortions, not merely as an alternative to the back alley but because it was lucrative. Had that aspect of his medical practice been widely known, it would have ostracized the family.

Silence guaranteed protection, and Eleanor learned how to keep secrets.

* * *

Intent on not living beneath her father's roof any longer, she enrolled at the local college, meeting her lifelong best friend, Lynn, in the admissions line. But academics bored Mom, and she dropped out to work as an insurance adjuster, saving enough within a year to make payments on a Studebaker convertible. On weekends, she cruised Wilshire Boulevard with Lynn, hoping to get *noticed*. Somehow they caught the attention of a window dresser for Neiman Marcus and were offered modeling contracts at twenty dollars a week.

Life was good—until they stumbled into their first marriages.

Lynn wed an attorney, and Eleanor got hitched to the man's law partner. They split after my eldest sister, Laurie, was born in 1955. The pressure of a newborn weighed on them, and Mom's persona proved too domineering for most men. Lynn's marriage was short-lived as well. Divorce left them broke and stigmatized as single mothers.

Eleanor had no choice but to move back home.

She started working as an extra, hustling all night in scantily clad ensembles on the set of *Around the World in 80 Days* while being yelled at by little men with enormous egos. It wasn't all drudgery, of course. During breaks, she met and made friends with other ingénues. But it was Lynn with whom Mom laughed the hardest and commiserated the most. They were cast in the same films alongside leading men like Marlon Brando, who flirted with Mom. When I was a kid, she'd get nostalgic whenever his movies came on TV.

"He was the nicest, sweetest man, Rafie. We'd sit down and talk, and oh, he'd want to know everything about me!" she'd recall.

I remember that sentiment clearly because it made Mom feel so important. My father, Ray, adored her but seldom expressed his feelings. I thought, *Marlon Brando. Wow. He's the type of guy I want to be.* Yet that ideal would elude me until my story started being less about what I wanted and more about what others deserved of me.

Most actors weren't as chivalrous as Brando. But for Mom and Lynn, rich and powerful men were hardly a threat. They were modest, and their chastity immunized the gals. The same big wheels who'd cast them as chorus girls would someday find themselves as regular guests at their dinner parties.

In the meantime, they were at a nadir, sifting through the wreckage of failed marriages. They'd become depressed about their prospects of finding true love, their financial instability, and the daunting responsibilities of raising children alone.

The pity party wouldn't last. Channeling the spontaneity that scored them their first entertainment gigs, they decided to try their luck in glitzy Manhattan. But their plans fell apart after Eleanor was called away to attend a baby shower for her cousin in the Emerald City.

* * *

In Seattle, Mom accidentally met the man of her dreams, my dad—*carefree* Ray Moscatel. Friends called him that because he cracked jokes like an insult comic and smiled like a Cheshire cat. It's how he coped, having been reared in an Orthodox Jewish household where disobedience was dealt with harshly. Ray was often banished to a dark basement for hours as a boy. When he could get away, he stayed out playing basketball until sundown, growing strong and tall.

There was a six-inch height difference between Dad and me. It should have been the giveaway that I'd been adopted. I resemble neither him nor my mother. But the only person who ever bothered to point out the obvious was Scotty.

He'd ask, "Hey, Bucky, how come you don't look like Uncle Ray?"

"Because I take after my mom," I'd explain.

"But you don't look like Auntie Ellie either," he'd reply.

Those frank observations took root in me, though I reflexively dismissed them at the time. And Dad's size wasn't the sole dissimilarity. My father had Turkish blood, chestnut eyes, and the jawline of a sultan. If you threw a fez on his noggin, you couldn't distinguish him from a native of Istanbul.

Me? I can't leave the house without sunscreen.

Ray was also a natural athlete. In 1949, following an outstanding collegiate career, he was invited to try out for the Boston Celtics. Tragically, he missed the opportunity when his father, an earnest man but a heavy smoker and workaholic, was stricken with leukemia. One afternoon, in his forties, he fell against a stack of boxes in the back of his mattress store and was found unconscious. Three days later, he was dead.

"Tell you one thing about my pop," Dad once shared poignantly. "In college, he'd never come to my games. Never. My mother would come, but never my dad. But this one time, we were in Corvallis, Oregon, for the quarterfinals of the NCAA. All of a sudden, I turned and saw him sitting there in the stands. He'd never come to a game. Never. I went up there, and I hugged him, and I kissed him. And a little after that, he died. But that was a big thrill for me to see him there, *just once*. I'll never forget it."

Ray took over his father's store at nineteen. He hated the business but kept the lights on until his younger brother could take the reins. Later, he purchased a watering hole on Capitol Hill, polishing shot glasses and hauling drunks off their barstools until the wee hours. Dad started drinking heavily on that job, an addiction that began to consume him about the time he was introduced to Eleanor.

The two met on a balmy Sunday at the baby shower. Ray had dropped off his little sister there and decided to stick around. He was sitting alone on the cedar porch, his spearpoint collar shirt unbuttoned, nursing a cold beer. Mom arrived late with her daughter in tow. As she touched the railing on the front steps, her eyes connected with Dad's—instant fireworks. Eleanor was the most desirable woman he'd ever seen, a Barbie doll in the flesh. He tipped his bottle toward her and ogled as she strutted into the house like a gazelle. They sparked up a conversation in the backyard and were married by month's end.

It wasn't the fairytale ending that Dr. Robert and Mama Rita had in mind for Eleanor. Still, they felt relieved that Laurie, their granddaughter, would have a two-parent home. And with little fanfare, the three Moscatels began their lives together in a craftsman bungalow on Lake Washington.

* * *

While cozy at first, the rain tapping endlessly on the sash windows was neither comforting nor inspiring to Mom. She took a chance and opened a boutique on the main drag in Seward Park, hoping to bring some of the styles she loved about LA to Seattle. But soon after her grand opening, she faced headwinds when the stuffy rabbi from Dad's synagogue stopped in.

"You are wife of Raymond?" the man inquired with a heavy accent as he picked through the unconventional garb on the racks.

"That's me," Eleanor replied with a friendly grin behind the cash register. "Thanks for coming in, Rabbi."

She knew he'd heard of her because he privately implored Dad to wait a few months before getting married to ensure she wasn't pregnant. He'd also refused to perform their ceremony. Nevertheless, Mom played nice.

"What do you think of the clothes?" she asked as he judged each item.

"Sephardim do not wear these things," he tersely remarked.

A few minutes later, he departed, leaving Mom demoralized. Before she knew it, foot traffic and sales dropped as women from the tight-knit community heeded the religious leader's warning to avoid *unorthodox* fashions. Eleanor was miffed and grew bored. She prayed for more excitement in her life.

Then, one day, God answered her prayers.

It was the holy Sabbath. Dad's tavern was closed, and he'd walked the mile to synagogue just as he had since he was a child. Men were seated on one side of the congregation and women on the other in those days. Mom purposely showed up ten minutes late for services that Saturday wearing one of the low-cut dresses the rabbi disapproved of.

"What are you doing, Eleanor?" Dad murmured as she sat beside him.

"What's it look like, Ray?" Mom replied, with everyone's eyes fixed on them.

She'd crossed the line, and her trespass triggered a roar of dissent. The women covered their mouths, tittering, as the men grumbled and pointed their fingers, condemning her. Dad began to squirm, adjusting his collar, beads of sweat forming beneath his receding hairline.

The rabbi picked up his prayer book and waived it over his head as he stomped down the aisle, yelling at Eleanor in Ladino, the Sephardic language. The congregation swelled behind him, surrounding Mom like a pitch-forked mob, demanding that she respect tradition and sit with the women! But Eleanor refused to bend the knee, sneering at the rabbi as she left.

Dad remained in his seat, unsure of what to do.

"Get off your ass, Raymond!" Mom shouted from the exit.

He stood up and followed her out of the synagogue, bombarded on both sides of the aisle by insulted congregants. A life of indentured servitude had begun.

* * *

Inevitably, the Moscatels shuttered the apparel shop and moved to Los Angeles, where Dad found a job stocking shelves in a grocery. But it wouldn't be enough to make ends meet, especially since they'd just had a second child, my brother Albert, born in 1958. Mom began acting again and booked a feature called *G.I. Blues*.

She'd heard stories about Elvis Presley, the star.

"He was not a lovely person. He made fun of people," she would say.

There was also his reputation with women. Presley moved on almost every pretty girl who passed his trailer, and they usually kissed him back. But while Eleanor wasn't a nun, she was no groupie. When Elvis pulled her into his dressing room and tried to plant one *on her*, she turned her face in disgust.

"Pig!" she cried out, resisting him.

"C'mon, baby," he cooed, hoping to calm her.

"No! What is wrong with you?" Mom retorted, freeing herself. "I'm a married woman."

"It's only a little kiss," he replied, taken aback by her rejection.

Had that harassment occurred today, Eleanor may have received a settlement check. But it was 1960, so instead, she was fired that afternoon by the King of Rock 'n' Roll.

Serendipitously, she was hired weeks later, with Lynn, on *Bonanza*, television's most popular series, featuring a young Michael Landon as Little Joe Cartwright. Mom's best friend bewitched the rising star. He pursued and romanced her, and they were married in 1963 when my brother Albert turned five. Eight years later, the Landons would light a candle at his bar mitzvah.

Michael was the embodiment of a mensch. On set, the actor was a typical perfectionist. But in the real world, he never refused an autograph, badgered a waiter, or used status to gain an advantage. Humility was at the core of his character from early in his boyhood. A bed-wetter into his teens, his mother would shame him by pinning his soiled sheets outside his window. He'd race home after school to stash them before the neighborhood kids could see.

And despite good looks and artistry, nothing came easy to the man. Like many entertainers back then, he was forced to change his name from Eugene Orowitz to the more regal-sounding *Michael Landon* to get work. He later carved out his niche in Hollywood, portraying upstanding Christian fathers and guardian angels. And like Eleanor, he didn't allow the pain of his past to prescribe his future.

* * *

Mom's work was steady on the western. But even if you were best friends with the star, extra work didn't make you millions. The Landons weren't rich, either. When they moved into their first house in Encino, they couldn't afford a dining room set. My parents would visit them and sit on egg crates as they served dinner.

Eventually, Michael's career did start earning him a fortune. Mom and Dad were happy for him and Lynn but understandably envious because they were still stuck in a Spanish duplex owned by Dr. Robert. The cost of living kept rising, and Mom knew something would have to give if they were to provide a better life for Laurie and Albert. But with her hands full raising kids and working long hours, it didn't leave much time for entrepreneurship.

Luckily, Mama Rita had something of her own brewing.

One afternoon, while Dad was driving her to an appointment, a billboard caught her eye from the passenger window—an ad for the Cleveland Chiropractic College.

"Chi-ro-prac-tor!" she exclaimed, her bright red lipstick stretching ear to ear.

"Thought I was taking you to the dentist," Dad said, weaving his tan Buick in and out of traffic, trying to change the subject.

Mama Rita shook her head, unleashing a string of expletives in her native language of Ladino, "*Ay, Ray. Eres un hadrozu, todo el tiempo murmuriandu. Carne con dos ojos!*"

She had called him *meat with two eyes!* But then, calming herself, gave the order in broken English, "You going to chi-ro-prac-tor school, Ray."

"I'm forty years old," he scoffed. "I ain't going back to school—"

"Oh, you going, Ray!" she commanded like a drill sergeant. "You going or else!"

"Or else what?"

"Or else I making Eleanor divorce you, *honey*," she threatened with a devilish grin.

"I ain't going!"

"Shh! No more talk," she instructed, putting a finger to her lips.

An hour later, after the dentist appointment, they pulled up in front of their duplex, and Dad opened the door for his mother-in-law. Mom was spread out on the couch, tired and glum.

"Eleanor, vonderful news!" Mama Rita trumpeted as she waltzed in, setting down her purse and removing her white gloves.

Mom sat up, interested. "What is it, Mama?"

"Ray has decided to go to chi-ro-prac-tor school. To be a doctor!" she declared as she pointed at Dad. "Isn't it right, Ray?"

Dad grunted. The matter was settled, and Mom was ecstatic.

Ray kept working a day shift at the grocery while attending night school. My father had enrolled two decades after getting his degree from Seattle University. Not an easy transition for a one-time star athlete. But those glory days were gone. He was now the oldest student in the class, and his teachers could care less whether he'd been All-State.

* * *

Upon graduation, Mom realized they'd need to hang a shingle if they were ever to make something of themselves. With the few bucks they'd saved from her acting work and a small loan from Dr. Robert, they started Banner Medical Clinic. Ray proved he had strong hands and healed his patients, yet success didn't come overnight. When they opened their first office in Inglewood, the one location they could afford, the carpenter they hired to build out the space threw cold water on their dream.

"Lady, you're gonna have a hard time makin' it. This city is swamped with chiropractors," he noted.

"You build the exam room, and I'll build the business," Eleanor shot back.

But the naysayer was onto something—there was no shortage of back doctors in Los Angeles. Still, there was bound to be demand with thousands of car accidents on the highways.

Why were some doing better than others? Mom wondered.

It didn't take her long to figure it out. Business wasn't just about providing a product or service. It was about relationships. Clients weren't walking into chiropractor offices right off the street—they were being referred after accidents. The Moscatels would need to hook up with a top-notch personal injury attorney. Only that way could they make a sizeable dent in the business.

But where was such a person to be found?

Mom checked her local paper, the *Los Angeles Times*. A young lawyer from Boyle Heights was often featured in the blotter, usually as an aggressive plaintiff's attorney for injured motorists and occasionally representing a jilted spouse. Eleanor decided to seek him out.

Without reservation, she strode down to his office building the following afternoon, took the elevator to the penthouse, and informed the receptionist that she had a meeting with *the barrister*.

"I don't see anything on his calendar, Miss—"

"*Mason*," my mother responded, smoothing out her pink suit.

She'd used the alias for the same reason Michael had—for work. Having gone by a few different stage names herself, she guessed using one in business might be helpful.

What are the chances a man like Donald Sterling would want to do business with a Moscatel? she thought, waiting in the reception.

Moscatel seemed so ethnic in comparison to Sterling. She wasn't embarrassed by the surname but wouldn't let it interfere with her plans. Dropping it was an acceptable sacrifice, she assured herself. She wasn't married to it, after all, just Ray. Little did Mom know Donald T. Sterling's moniker wasn't authentic, either. The "T" stood for Tekowitz.

She grew impatient as the phones rang off the hook, and the receptionist struggled to juggle the calls.

"I'm sorry, Miss Mason. I can't find your appointment. Would you like to wait?"

"No, that's okay," Mom replied, advancing toward Sterling's office.

The receptionist popped up on her toes and tried to stop Mom's beeline but couldn't block her charge. Mom flung open his door, and Don lowered his reading glasses.

"Hello," he said, pleasantly surprised.

"Hello," Mom replied, uncertain what to say next.

"I'm sorry, Mr. Sterling. I told Miss Mason she needed an appointment," said the receptionist, clinging to the doorframe.

Eleanor was statuesque in heels and held her ground like a matador.

"It's fine. I've got a few minutes," Don said, inviting her to sit.

As the secretary retreated, Mom parked it in front of his desk.

"How can I help you, *Miss Mason?*"

"Well. I have a new chiropractic office."

"Okay," said Don, tilting back in his chair and cupping his hands behind his head.

"Uh, what do you think about sending me some business?"

Don laughed, admiring her chutzpah. He cleared his schedule and gave her an hour.

Over the next few years, they would develop a symbiotic relationship. Banner Medical expanded and opened satellite locations in Pasadena and South Central. Don would send her new clients, and Mom identified residential properties for Sterling, who was pivoting to real estate. Before the end of the century, he'd become the wealthiest private landlord in the city, from the Wilshire Corridor to Koreatown.

Eventually, Mom and Dad saved enough bread for their own place. They'd had three kids by then, the youngest an almond-eyed baby with frizzy hair—my sister Marleigh, born in 1970. After her first birthday, they moved from the duplex to Beverly Hills.

Mom took Don's sage advice to buy the worst home in the best neighborhood, which happened to be across the street from his. The down payment was every dollar my parents could scrounge. Happy but house-poor, Eleanor signed up for free drawing classes at the adult education center to fill the space. Her paintings, copies of 19th-century impressionism, still hang on the walls.

Lynn and Michael followed the Moscatels to Beverly Hills from Encino and purchased a sprawling estate up the road. As our two families grew close, Michael began producing a show about an American frontier family that would forever change my life.

He called it *Little House on the Prairie.*

* * *

Though he was the biggest star on television, talk of "the business" wasn't the predominant conversation among Michael's closest friends. He rarely mentioned work when in Mom and Dad's company. They weren't industry people, so they got to know a markedly different side of the man. One night, he'd be walking the red carpet, blinded by Kodak flashes, and the next morning he'd be helping Dad hook up a washer. Now and then, he'd even mow our front lawn, sometimes shirtless. Folks would drive by and do double-takes.

They celebrated every occasion together. And for Mom's 40th birthday, Michael gave her a special present. He arranged for her to be a contestant on the game show *Hollywood Squares.* Michael would be the "secret square" that night, and Mom was to pretend as if she didn't know him from Adam.

Before the cameras rolled, they conspired. It was half-hearted—more of a prank between old friends than anything else.

"Eleanor, now listen to me carefully," he explained. "When the host gives me a question, I'm going to do this with my ear," he said, scratching his lobe. "I'll do that if I know the answer and you agree, okay?"

"Uh-huh," Mom nodded.

"Sure you got this, Eleanor?" he asked, knowing how absent-minded she could be.

"Michael. Please. *You can trust me,*" she winked.

"Okay, now act like we've never met," he said, walking away toward an attractive makeup artist.

Mom performed well during the first half of the matchup and had momentum going into the final round, when she picked Michael, the "secret square," for the win.

The host swiveled in his chair and read from an index card.

"Okay. Michael Landon. For the win. Which of these actors plays the Argentine mercenary Che Guevara in the new film *Bloody Che Contra*? Is it Francisco Rabal, Steve McQueen, or Robert Redford?"

Michael restated the question so Mom could see him scratching at his ear and answered confidently, "Rabal. Francisco Rabal."

"Are you sure?" asked the host.

"Hundred percent," Michael confirmed, scratching his ear again conspicuously.

It wasn't a tough one. Everyone watching knew that neither Robert Redford nor Steve McQueen, two blonds with light complexions, could have possibly played Che Guevara.

The host turned to Mom. "Eleanor. For the win. Agree or disagree?"

But in all the excitement, she'd become distracted and forgotten the sign.

After a nail-biting pause, she leaned into the mic, answering meekly, "I'll disagree."

"Oh, no! Not correct, Eleanor. Not correct. It was Rabal. Francisco Rabal," the host jeered as the camera panned in on Michael slapping his forehead.

Ray couldn't believe the blunder and never let her live it down. He and Michael poked fun at Eleanor unremittingly, especially when drinking. And while they were typically happy drunks, their compulsions would one day get the best of them.

* * *

A year after Mom lost the gameshow, the Landons invited the Moscatels to a Vegas banquet. Ray excused himself from Michael's table to take a leak. At the urinal, he glanced over, and standing beside him was his idol—the one man who could leave him speechless, the Chairman of the Board, Frank Sinatra. Dad gaped at him with his mouth open like a junkyard dog. Frank recoiled, feigning disgust.

"What are you looking at, pal?" he asked Ray in a scary, low voice.

Dad retrained his sights on the urinal, red-faced.

It was 1972. Paramount's *The Godfather* had just been released, featuring a scene with a character purportedly based on Sinatra and strongly implying he was mafioso. Ray didn't want to take any chances.

"Hey, I'm sorry about that. I—"

"Kidding, pal. Kidding," Frank laughed, zipping his pants. "You out there with Mikey?"

Dad nodded.

"Good. Tell him I'll swing by after the show. Nice to meet ya," he told his biggest fan.

Dad still had his mouth wide open as Frank was handed a towel by the bemused restroom attendant and left.

When he returned to the table, Sinatra was on stage, and a Nevada senator was sitting with Michael. Ray, who knew all about sports but nothing about politics, spent the night getting hammered with the legislator. He woke up the next morning hungover and sprawled on a satin couch in Michael's suite.

Walking through the casino later that afternoon, the two buddies ran into the politician.

"Fine talking to you fellas last night," he said, lighting a cigar. "You have some interesting ideas about this country, Ray."

"Thank you," Dad responded.

"Keep 'em to yourself," the senator added, pointing at him accusatorily.

As his handlers whisked him away, Michael raised his eyebrows.

"What on earth did you say to that man, Raymond?"

"Who gives a shit?" my father shrugged. "Let's go play some cards."

* * *

It wouldn't be the Moscatels' last foray into politics.

A couple of years later, in 1974, Eleanor campaigned for Jerry "Moonbeam" Brown in the California gubernatorial race. She'd worked hard to organize fundraisers for him and line up donors. But during one event, he'd made the mistake of parking his light blue, beat-up Plymouth in her driveway. Normally, that wouldn't have been a problem, but it had just been paved. And Jerry had been reminded politely *and* repeatedly to leave it on the street.

Laurie came home earlier than usual that afternoon, and when she tried to pull her Firebird in, couldn't get around Jerry's wheels. So she hopped out and barged into the entry but was restrained by a couple of his lackeys.

"Hey, where you think you're goin', young lady?" one asked, accosting her.

"Who are you two goons?" Laurie hissed, tilting her aviators.

"The Secretary of State is inside—invitation only."

My sister cocked her head and snickered, "Invitation?"

"Yeah," said the other, adjusting his stance.

"I don't need an invitation to my own house, assholes," she cursed, brushing them aside.

She found Mom in the living room stirring an olive martini, cornered by the candidate.

"Laurie! What are you doing home, darling?" said Eleanor.

"We have a little problem, Mother," her daughter replied.

Mom pinched her arm, introducing her to their guest of honor. He apologized for the confusion at the door and promised to move his Plymouth. Yet hours later, as my parents bid him farewell on their front porch, he had still not moved that damn car.

"Can't thank you enough, Eleanor," the candidate said, shaking Mom's hand.

"Really, it was our pleasure," Mom replied gleefully, waving as he walked to his vehicle.

Albert peered down at them from behind sheer curtains in the window above. He'd spent the day holed up in his bedroom spinning *Supertramp* LPs. Laurie walked in and leaned up against her little brother.

"That Plymouth looks kind of old," observed Albert.

Jerry got behind the wheel and put on his belt, waving one last time at Mom.

"Something's not right about that guy, Eleanor," Dad mumbled, chewing his toothpick.

As soon as Jerry drove off, Mom's mood soured.

Moonbeam had left a big puddle in her driveway!

She unstrapped her heels, handed them to Ray, and approached it like a homicide detective. Bending down, she ran a finger through to check if it was maybe from the radiator—but it was oil! And, in that instant, without a second thought, she decided that "son of a bitch" would never set foot in her house again.

You simply do not park in Eleanor Moscatel's driveway, leave an oil stain, and expect to be invited back—*even if you are the next Governor of California.*

* * *

The Moscatel family, neither politicians nor old money nor celebrities, had ensconced themselves in Beverly Hills. They'd been auditioned and cast in this rags-to-riches fable, far from the poverty and struggles they'd once known. But that story was destined to take a sharp and dreadful turn. While attending a screening of *Little House on the Prairie* in 1975, they received a call from the chief resident in the emergency room.

A monster lay waiting at their gates.

Tragedies

That fateful evening, *Remember Me,* an episode, of all things, about adoption, was screened at Paramount Studios. The Moscatels were usually invited to those events, but the Landons couldn't find a space for Albert that night.

It's how Eleanor recalled it, at least, which didn't make sense to her because Michael was the showrunner. So when she spotted Lynn's coiffeur sitting in the audience, Mom nearly lost it.

How could they deny my son and seat that man in his place? she asked herself.

It was one of many questions that would go unanswered in the sorrowful days that followed my brother's death. It's the nature of tragedy. The emotional upheaval of loss blurs a survivor's memory. And their grief, from denial to bouts of anger, guilt, bargaining, and ultimately acceptance, often ends with a little piece of them dying too.

* * *

Albert, who left this world a year before I was born, was canonized like a Catholic saint in our home. Portraits of him in sterling silver frames, watching me with his commanding eyes, were displayed in every room. His soft brown hair was cut like a Beatles mop-top, but he grew it long the year before he'd have come of age. And when he popped his collar, you could mistake him for a young John Travolta. He was everything I wasn't—a chess champion, star student, and cotillion dancer, loved by all.

And unlike me, Albert never got in that much trouble. He so seldomly veered off course that Mom could cite each infraction. His first criminal act, aged seven, was stealing a Mother's Day card from the local drugstore. Ray drove him back to the shop and made him apologize to the manager. In a second instance, our sultry neighbor caught him peeping on her with a telescope he'd received for his tenth birthday. *She wasn't even naked.* But Albert's worst offense by far was lobbing an egg at a police cruiser from his balcony as a teen. For that, he was severely reprimanded—although he was aiming for Dad's Buick. Every other recollection of him was related to me like a treasured anecdote.

Given his good nature, it's hard to discern Michael and Lynn's motive for not letting Albert attend the screening. It wasn't malicious, but I can't fathom it was as simple as not having enough seats. My father thought it may have been due to a girl in the production on whom Albert had developed a crush. Perhaps Michael was trying to keep them apart, or maybe my brother didn't want to go in the first place.

Whatever the reason, Albert drove alone to a house party that evening. After stepping outside to get marijuana from the trunk of his car, he was struck violently by a speeding Volkswagen bug. Hearing the accident, horrified guests spilled out and surrounded my brother, whose head had hit the asphalt and was bleeding. An ambulance arrived ten minutes later and rushed him to the hospital.

When the call came into the studio that Albert had been admitted, Mom bellowed—a cry so loud it could be heard beyond the padded soundstage. She ran out with Dad. By the time they'd arrived at Albert's bedside, he'd already lost consciousness.

My oldest sister, Laurie, his best friend and confidant, had been on a date to the drive-in that evening. Albert asked to join her, but she didn't want her little brother hanging around.

"Any other night but that one, I would have loved to be with him," she confessed over the phone as I was writing this book, not having spoken much about the calamity before.

She'd learned he was hurt after having a premonition at the theater. When she called home from a payphone to check in, our housekeeper delivered the bad news that Albert was in a coma. Laurie and her date raced to the hospital, blowing through every stoplight.

When their car hit the curb at the ER, my sister sprang out, leaving the passenger door ajar and bolting through the lobby to the elevator. She punched the buttons, trying to call it down to no avail, and searched for the stairwell but was so frantic she didn't realize it was right behind her. When the elevator doors finally split open, two figures stood before her—Dad and Michael, embracing and weeping.

She was too late. Her brother was dead.

Laurie went into shock from the catastrophic loss. She collapsed on her bed when she came home from the hospital in the early morning. Awakening that afternoon, she briefly sat up at the edge of her mattress before crossing to the window overlooking our driveway. As she peeled back the curtains, she noticed Albert's car parked where it normally would be, unaware a friend had driven it back home.

For a fleeting moment, she presumed she'd had a nightmare. She darted down the hallway into her brother's room and saw a body his size, with the same thick mane, lying face down on the sheets.

"Albert. You're alive!" Laurie screamed as she jumped onto his torso.

But when he flipped over, she burst into tears—it was just a cousin from Seattle who'd come in on the redeye.

Laurie never really stopped crying after that.

And as for Eleanor and Ray, like any parents facing a tribulation of that magnitude, watching their child suffer was unbearable. It felt like a nuclear bomb had dropped. Nothing would be the same again. The way they'd remember their lives would be permanently divided between what happened before Albert took his last breath and the days afterward. At his funeral, as the coffin was being lowered, Eleanor jumped into her son's grave, kissing his casket and wailing in distress. She had to be lifted out and restrained by my father.

* * *

The Sterling and Landon families were also devastated by Albert's death, particularly Michael Landon, who'd been so close to Mom and Dad. He never spoke publicly of the incident but added a new character to the show and named him after the boy as a tribute.

My brother's memory, through the character of Albert Ingalls, would live on in *Little House on the Prairie* for another six seasons and syndication to this day. As a kid, each time I caught a rerun, it reminded me of someone I could never be. My jealousy fed the monster. It laughed as I carried Albert's name, my middle one, like a ship's anchor. Though I was loved, the specter of my brother would haunt me for the better part of my life, and measuring up to his legacy felt nerve-wracking.

* * *

Seeking solace in the year following his death, Mom sought fortune-tellers and mystics, talking to anyone who claimed they could reach her son on the other side. But it was futile, and she was a shell of her former self. Nothing could console her. She cried so much that her face became swollen, as if she'd gone twelve rounds with a boxer.

As the days wore on, darkness enveloped the once gleaming canopy above our home. The haze was like the ash from a massive volcano, blocking the sunlight and killing all the dreams planted in its fertile garden. Even the gardenia bushes outside Mom's window didn't seem to smell as sweet as they once had. She rarely left the house.

Luckily, she had a friend in her corner who wouldn't give up on her—a bombastic socialite I'd come to know as Miss Dottie. While heavy-set, the woman moved like an angel, one you might find bathing in the clouds of a fresco on a cathedral ceiling. I remember her dancing across our living room like a blind ballerina, belting standards and lightening any mood.

A year after Albert died, Miss Dottie heard through the grapevine that a young, unmarried woman in her neighborhood had become pregnant. The girl's father was livid when he found out the circumstances and beseeched his daughter to get rid of the baby by any means necessary. Eleanor, no longer of child-bearing age, began considering adoption after talking with Miss Dottie about the situation. Nothing would bring Albert back, yet the thought of pitter-patter around the house was one thing that made Mom feel better.

Six months later, I was delivered to the Moscatels, wrapped like a present with a ribbon tying me to the past.

Comedies

Three years after my adoption, Eleanor and Ray renewed their vows in Acapulco. Michael Landon, dressed in his white V-neck and jeans, officiated. And as our families gathered on the beach at sundown, the actor turned to me, dancing ring-around-the-Rosie with his daughters. He made a goofy face, and I smiled, my two front teeth bigger than a beaver's.

"Good God. Look at the size of those things," he jested.

Despite his happy-go-lucky veneer, Michael had a lot on his mind. Aside from a faltering marriage, he was muddling through the season closer for *Little House on the Prairie.* The script was written but missing something BIG.

"Come here, kiddo," he shouted my way.

I ran happily toward him. He gave Dad the Gideon Bible he'd been holding and hoisted me, examining my teeth like an orthodontist.

"I think we're going to have to start calling you *Bucky,*" Michael teased.

Everybody laughed, and the nickname stuck. A week later, he cast me in the show's finale. In my only scene, I wander off with another toddler during a wedding. After she innocently kisses me, Michael steps into the frame and swoops her up.

"Ah, you're going to wait until you're eighteen, little lady," he says in a fatherly tone.

"But I love her," my character whimpers.

It marked the beginning and end of my television career. But when it was over, Michael escorted me across the set to my parents as if I were a star.

"Thanks, Bucky," he said, tipping his cowboy hat.

* * *

It's no surprise that the Moscatels let their friends call me names. They were thick-skinned and taught me that sometimes the more you laugh, the less you cry. As kids, we weren't allowed to mope around the house with a sourpuss's face for more than twenty-four hours. *It was a rule.* And there were no safe spaces in the peanut gallery we called home. We raised our voices, fought like raccoons, and occasionally called the cops on one another.

And while we said things we'd come to regret, I've learned that remorse keeps you grounded. Whenever I hear somebody preaching about a life with no regrets, it sounds like I'm either listening to the story of Jesus or a liar. Everybody has regrets. You grow by taking an inventory of them, making amends, and not being offended whenever you're the butt of a joke.

But laughter isn't always the answer. And it wasn't enough for Mom to ward off the agony that ate away at her for years after losing her son. My adoption was a life preserver that kept our family afloat but couldn't calm the storm left in the wake of Albert's tragedy. Somehow we'd all make it to shore. But it would be long before the clouds passed, the sun came back out, and we could laugh again.

The reprieve Eleanor felt after my adoption didn't last. She began to direct blame toward Ray for what happened to Albert. She'd amassed several reasons to divorce him, stemming from his drinking. But Mom could never get over the loss of her first son. She convinced herself the only way to move on from the tragedy would be to get the closest thing reminding her of it out of her life for good—Dad.

I was six when they divorced.

A year later, she married *The King of Ribs.*

* * *

She met the restaurateur Tony Roma at the Playboy Mansion. Having already made a name for himself with his Texas barbecue joints, he'd started developing *Tony Roma's* into an international brand. But he was shy around women. It took some goading from a friend before he got the gumption to ask Mom out.

Marleigh and I peeked through the velvet curtains in our living room the first time Tony dropped her off after a date. He ran around the car like a teenager, opening the door of his black Porsche, taking her hand, and walking her up the steps. But when he leaned in for a goodnight kiss, she refused him.

"I'm not ready, Tony."

"Yeah, okay," he said, scratching his head. "What are you doing tomorrow?"

"Isn't that kind of soon?"

"I gotta see you again, Eleanor," he professed.

"Tony, I'm flying to Colorado in the morning with Lynn. Maybe—"

"Some other time," he said, finishing her sentence. "No problem, Eleanor."

She felt sorry for him, but two days later, he showed up unannounced in Aspen, stalking her through a display window as she shopped for a mink.

"Have you ever taken a horse-drawn sled?" Tony asked as she met him outside with her shopping bags.

"No," Eleanor answered, thinking of Ray, who'd never done anything so romantic.

"C'mon. You'll love it."

He blushed as the snow fell lightly on his fleece.

"When?" she inquired.

"How about right now?" he suggested.

Mom was smitten and took him up on the offer but still didn't let him in the front door for months. Once she did, their courtship was swift, with nuptials taking place at the Sands Hotel in Vegas two weeks after he proposed.

I'd never been to a wedding. I looked around at the strange faces surrounding us. It was the first time my two sisters and I had an opportunity to meet Tony's *family*. I can't recall much, but when I thumb through the wedding albums from that occasion, they look more like FBI reconnaissance photos. Even the servers looked like they'd killed people. Ray was probably willing to fight for Mom, but he knew his fists were no match for Tony's entourage.

Outnumbered or outgunned, he kept his distance.

Then one rainy April morning, Dad was seething as he picked me up from the house. He'd started losing more of his hair and looked beat. I slid into the passenger seat of his new Cadillac, where a towel was placed so I wouldn't soil the leather. My father was a man of few words, but I sensed he wanted a full report on the chef.

"He wears a lotta cologne," I complained.

"Uh-huh."

"And he cooks. A lot. All the time."

"Yeah, so what? What about your mother?"

"She's good."

"No, she's not. What is she saying? She misses me?"

"I think so, Dad," I speculated.

I couldn't be sure, but I hated how things had turned out for us. Life now had two plotlines instead of one. I wanted my story back to how it used to be, no matter how imperfect the characters in it were.

Dad pulled into the mall and hit the brakes in front of the barricade arm at the entrance.

"What is this?" he said, staring like a gorilla at a ticket machine that had replaced the parking attendant.

Those were new back then, and Ray had never used one. As he reached out to press the button, he noticed a suspicious man in black slacks and a white dress shirt approaching through the windshield.

"Hey, mister," the guy said, coming closer.

Dad put the car in park.

"This stupid thing. Can you believe it? Forgot to give me one of those when I came through," he blathered, looking at Dad's ticket dangling from the dispenser. "Mind if I grab another?"

"What?" asked Dad, perplexed.

"Oh, it spits out another if you're worried about it, mister," he said, tapping his fingers on the Cadillac's vinyl roof.

Ray wasn't good with technology but had been around the block long enough to smell bullshit. The man didn't want to pay the lost ticket fee.

"No," said Dad. "That's not how it works."

As they began to argue, I sank into my seat, feeling tension rise. My father tried to remain cool. But when the man attempted to steal the ticket, Dad lost it. He caught the thief's wrist and punched him in the nose. The guy collapsed, and Ray swung open his car door, smashing it repeatedly against the crook. While he lay on the curb, groaning, my father composed himself.

The parking ticket dislodged and floated down onto the man's bloodied shirt. Dad picked it up, closed the door, and put a hand back on the steering wheel.

"It's okay, Rafie. Don't be scared. He was asking for it," he said, patting my leg and driving in.

I was too afraid to open my eyes, fearing Ray more than I ever had that morning. And yet, I still wanted him back home because although he wasn't the father of the year, *at least he loved me.* Tony wasn't the worst stepdad, but he was an imposter—a hopeless romantic. He was only willing to put up with Marleigh and me until he could ship us off to boarding school.

* * *

Not long after the wedding, the chef immediately got to work remodeling our kitchen. But while his interior design and cooking talents wowed Mom, she could tell I wasn't into him.

She suggested we share a hobby.

Tony took the initiative and bought a miniature billiards table for us, setting it up beside the industrial-size ovens he'd just installed. The next morning he spent hours trying to teach me to shoot pool. I wasn't any good. *What seven-year-old is?* Still, Tony was patient because he was so damn crazy about Mom. And yet the more paternal he tried to act, the more I realized how much I missed my real father.

I tried everything to sabotage their marriage, even gaslighting Tony by hiding his Rolex or rolling back the date on its dial. He'd lose his mind trying to figure out what happened. And each day, I'd talk up Dad, too, begging Mom to take him back. Within months, I'd gotten Tony thrown out of the house not once but twice over fights related to Dad. He must have sensed Ray was her true love because the chef became less passionate each time he returned. The new marriage was soon on the rocks, the same way Mom liked her vodka.

As Tony leaned against our new kitchen cabinetry, chalking his pool cue that day, I could tell his Sicilian blood was boiling. I kept screwing up and scuffing the brand-new table.

"Watch the corner, son. Watch the corner," he repeated as he prepared to sink the eight ball, winking at me like the suave Casanova Mom had fallen for.

But I just couldn't stand listening to that motherfucker call me his *son*. I was only one man's son. And that man was Ray Moscatel.

Tony took his final shot, but right before it rolled into the pocket, I picked it up and chucked it at him as hard as I could, hitting him smack in the face.

"Why you—I'll kill you, you little punk!" he hollered, covering his left eye.

I gave him both middle fingers, yelped, and dove under the table as he came for me. He kneeled, yanking the pool stick out from my hands, and gave chase. I escaped beneath his hairy arms as he reached for me, circling the kitchen island with the fryers going. He caught my sleeve, but I broke loose and ran upstairs to my mother's room.

It must have been before noon because I could see through the balusters as I approached that her door was still shut.

"Mom! Help!" I cried, pounding on it.

Tony caught up to me, his eye starting to swell. As he raised the pool cue as if to strike me, my mother swung open the door wearing her curlers.

"Tony! What is the meaning of all this?"

"Look at my face, Eleanor!" he said, catching his breath.

"He's trying to kill me, Mom! He said he's going to kill me!" I pouted, wrapped around her knees like a frightened little cub and giving the chef my stink eye.

Mom crossed her arms as I lay at her slippers, weeping crocodile tears. She knew I was culpable but had already decided she wanted Ray back.

"What did you do to him, Tony?"

"What did *I* do? He threw an eight-ball at my face, Eleanor! At my face!" Tony yelled, gesturing toward his eye.

Mom shooed me inside and calmly pointed at her husband.

"Can I give you some advice, Tony?

"Advice?" he said, furrowing his brow.

"Yeah. Get your pots and pans and get the hell out of my house."

And with that churlish farewell, she slammed the door, exhaled, and began unrolling her curlers. Tony moved out for the final time that afternoon.

I guess it's true what they say—third time's the charm.

* * *

Meanwhile, up the street, Lynn Landon had become dispirited, suffering through a blistering divorce of her own from Michael. The lovers had settled into a storybook home with four loving kids—a picturesque life to any outsider. But it wasn't enough for Michael. He wanted to start all over with a younger woman. Lynn tolerated his indiscretion, hoping it was casual. But sex was his Achilles heel, and lust overtook him. He became racked with guilt and left her. The affair tarnished the actor's reputation as a family man and frayed the relationship between him and my parents, who sided with Lynn.

"Michael Landon was a marvelous father and loyal friend, Rafie, but a better actor than he ever was a husband," Mom told me.

Lynn went into a tailspin and never remarried. She took Michael to the cleaners, but alimony couldn't replace her lifelong investment in him. She retained custody of their children. And to heal what was left of her soul, Lynn joined a local church.

Bearing witness to her best friend's restoration, Eleanor figured it couldn't hurt to seek some salvation. She was lost at sea and caught in the riptide of a midlife crisis. We began attending church with Lynn and her children every Sunday. And after a few sermons, Mom was so inspired that she decided to break from the jet set to study scripture.

She devoured book after book, trying to untangle the mess left inside her by one tumultuous marriage after another and her son's tragic death. Western religion, Eastern mysticism, self-help, Khalil Gibran—you name it, Mom tried it. But our time living as Christians remains the most tranquil I can remember all my life.

The church also helped Eleanor recognize that if God were to be welcomed into our lives, her monster would have to be shown the door. That monster took many forms and often showed up at night with a bottle of Smirnoff. It was an addiction that kept my parents from dealing with their marital problems. But when a church elder encouraged Mom to attend Alcoholics Anonymous, she hesitated. Then, upon Lynn's urging, she reconsidered and agreed to go once or twice to see if it was worth it.

These were the days of the big smokey rooms overflowing with recovering drunks of every race, creed, and color. I relished the opportunity to accompany Mom to her meetings. You could sit in the back of those rooms and hear the sort of Frankenstein tales even Mary Shelley couldn't have written. They made the fiendish monster chasing me feel less threatening, if but for an hour.

The first time I saw Mom share at a meeting, we'd been going to AA for maybe a week. She spoke after a bald guy in a grimy tank top she'd been sitting beside.

"Hello, everyone!" she said as if they were guests at her cocktail party.

The room hushed.

"Tell us your name," the man in the dirty shirt said, taking a drag from his smoke.

"My what?" she asked, fairly new to the program.

"Your name," he repeated.

"Oh, yes," she said, beaming her thousand-watt smile. "I'm Eleanor."

"Hi, Eleanor," the room replied in unison.

"Tell 'em you're an alcoholic," prompted the man.

"Oh, no. I don't have a drinking problem," Mom said, nervously laughing. "I'm here because of my ex-husband, Ray. He's the real alcoholic."

"Lady, you're looking for Al-Anon. Down the hall," the man said, shaking his head.

"Excuse me, sir," Mom scolded him. "As I was about to say, my husband was driving us home—drunk. I'll admit that I had a few, too. We began to argue, and I made him pull over on the freeway, got out, and walked down the offramp to this restaurant. I just needed a glass of water."

As we listened, I covered my face.

"They refused, so I asked to see the owner, *Wendy*," Mom continued. "Her name was in big red letters on the door. They demanded I leave, and well, I was humiliated."

Mom opening up to a roomful of strangers seemed so out of character, but her vulnerability must have been cathartic. She looked relieved.

"It's given me time to think," she finished. "And I've decided, you know, enough! *From now on, I'm only going to drink if it's a really special occasion.*"

You could hear a pin drop.

Then, as she sat down, a granny in a Mickey Mouse sweater looked up from way in the back and asked, "What? I didn't hear. What restaurant did she say it was?"

"*Wendy's*!" everyone shouted.

Laughter swallowed the room, but Mom didn't get her own joke. To be fair, *Wendy's* was a popular franchise, but Eleanor Moscatel wasn't their target customer.

I remembered that awful day a little differently.

Before hopping on the freeway, my parents had bought me a bouncy ball from the supermarket. They'd been squabbling the whole afternoon. As Dad careened down the carpool lane in our wood-paneled Mercury station wagon, I watched the cars behind us. I couldn't stand hearing them argue about Dad's drinking again and wanted to break up their fight. So, I rolled down the back window and tossed the ball out. Dad caught me doing it in his rearview and flew into a rage as it bounced across the lanes behind us like a giant ping-pong ball. He started cursing, and Mom forced him to pull the car onto the shoulder.

That fight continued for weeks.

I sometimes think the silver lining to all that drunken mayhem may have been that I was adopted. If there's a genetic disposition for that disease, I likely dodged it. But my monster didn't care about where my misery originated. It would feed off any trace of it to steer me toward other destructive behavior.

* * *

Mom talked Dad into joining AA shortly after getting her thirty-day sobriety chip. Once he'd earned his chip, she persuaded him to attend church. Ray wanted her back so desperately that he was willing to try anything. Before long, he'd gotten sober, moved back in, and was wearing that Rolex I'd hidden from Tony.

The Landon and Sterling girls were happy to see Dad back, almost as much as I was. They loved their Uncle Ray. He'd make a point of parking his Cadillac on the street each weekend so they could roller-skate in the driveway with Marleigh. I often tried to join the fun with my bike but was avoided like the plague. They were thirteen-year-old girls, and who could blame them? All I could do was hone my espionage skills and wait for an opportunity to tattle.

It came one day when I heard about *the beatdown.*

The girls had huddled around Marleigh, glued to her every word about a rumor. Two of the toughest eighth-graders in school would be meeting after the bell to settle a score. It was all anybody could talk about, but the details were sketchy. Everybody knew the time. Nobody knew the place.

"I heard everything!" I spouted prematurely from behind Mom's gardenia bush.

The girls' heads swung around. They stared at me like I was *carne con dos ojos*. I jumped off my bicycle and took a few steps back as they skated toward me. Soon I was up against an iron gate, and they were in my grill.

"You say something, Bucky?" Marleigh asked, balancing between her girlfriends.

I shook with fear but bravely stuttered, "I know about *the b-b-beatdown*."

"Yeah. So what?" one of her girlfriends clapped back.

"Well. I wanna go. And if you don't take me, I'm gonna tell Mom!"

Marleigh took the threat seriously. She couldn't risk being the only kid in class to miss the most talked about social event of the semester.

"Okay," she capitulated. "But don't be anywhere near me when it happens."

I nodded, and they skated away like a roller-derby gang.

The following Monday, we learned the beatdown would occur in the alley behind the school. Marleigh planned to ask Dad to pick us up late so we could watch the fight, but there was a problem. Mom had recently hired a nice fellow named Serafin as our driver—and he'd been instructed to bring us home right after classes, with no exceptions.

"Serafin?" my sister asked from the backseat, flustered.

"Yes, Misses Marleigh?" he responded, wearing a tiny chauffeur cap.

"Serafin, I have to go somewhere before you take us back to the house."

"No, Misses Marleigh," he said, shaking his head in the rearview mirror of Dad's Cadillac. "Señora say you go home."

I sat beside my big sister on the sticky leather seat, watching her hopes dashed. But from how she was fidgeting, I could tell she wasn't ready to give up just yet.

"Serafin?"

"Yes, Misses Marleigh?"

"I know *exactly* what you're doing back in that little room my mother gave you to sleep."

She was bluffing and had no idea if he was up to anything nefarious, but she just had to go to that beatdown! Poor Serafin must have been guilty of something because he immediately flipped the Cadillac around and pulled it into the alley as directed.

As our car inched toward the venue, Marleigh rolled down her window. A mob of bloodthirsty kids gathered around the two amateur pugilists, egging them on. I climbed over my sister's lap to get a better view.

"Get down!" she said, pushing me away.

A boy standing on his tiptoes at the edge of the crowd turned to us, recognizing Marleigh. They were in the same grade but had never spoken. I watched as she addressed him in her high-pitched voice.

"Excuse me. Robert?"

"Hi," the boy replied, surprised she was speaking to him.

It was as if she was about to ask for *Grey Poupon.*

"Is this where the beatdown is?"

"The what?" he responded, seeing my head pop up. "Oh. You mean the fight?"

Marleigh pushed me back again and stepped outside to join Robert. Serafin rolled up the tinted window and blocked my view. It was over in a matter of seconds.

As the crowd dispersed, my sister hopped back in the car, and I squinted at the loser—beaten, bloodied, and crying, alone in the alley.

The brutality of that image beset me. I'd seen violence before on television and from my father, yet the victims were usually adults. But that boy writhing in pain was only a little older than I was. Marleigh was disturbed by it, too. As she sat there with her eyes closed, I scooched over and held her hand, knowing we'd just seen a monster that wasn't under our bed.

* * *

I was relieved when we returned to church that Sunday.

We'd left Lynn's congregation in favor of a smaller fellowship that met in a middle school auditorium. I'll never forget showing up that first day and the heavenly brunette at the literature table in the foyer. It was actress Connie Sellecca. She played a lead on my favorite sitcom, *The Greatest American Hero.* I fell in love, ready to accept the Savior, right there on the spot.

As we walked down the aisle into the service, a pianist in the orchestra pit led the congregation in song. It was Connie's husband, John Tesh, host of *Entertainment Tonight.* I couldn't stop staring at him because *ET* was a staple in Los Angeles households. For a minute, my whole world felt a lot smaller and more connected. When John's melody faded, Pastor Louis took the pulpit. He was fastidious with combed red hair, a bulbous nose, and gold spectacles. But before his sermon could commence, I was carted off to Sunday school.

By then, my oldest sister Laurie had moved out and was an avowed atheist. Whatever faith she may have had died the night she lost her brother. My other sister, Marleigh, sat politely with my folks during service. Every Sunday, the church would ask a little more of Mom and Dad, who paid their tithings. But there was always one problem holding up our membership.

Raymond.

Dad was having trouble making the leap of faith. One weekend, I heard him calling Michael for support. He'd just begun producing *Highway to Heaven,* about a dapper angel sent to help the modern man.

But while Michael may have played Christians on TV, he was a Jew in real life.

"You're putting me on, Raymond," I overheard him chuckle.

"No. He'll be here any minute," said Dad, lighting a cigarette.

"Have you been honest with her?" Michael asked.

"You know that doesn't work with Eleanor," Dad replied.

Right then, the doorbell rang. I stopped eavesdropping, ran to my room, and pulled back the curtains. The pastor was standing outside, tapping his Bible. Seconds later, Marleigh burst into my room with a stack of RL Stine, Clive Barker, and Stephen King novels. She'd recently gotten braces and headgear and was talking with a lisp.

"Rafie. Hide *thith*," she said panicky, shoving her books into my arms.

"What? Why?" I asked.

"Because *Lou-ith ith* here," she said, hyperventilating.

"Is he coming to baptize us?"

"No, I don't *think-tho*. Not today."

"Why's he here then?"

"I heard him tell Mom we have to get rid of everything in the *howth* that *ithen't*—Look, I can't *exthplain* right now. *Jutht* hide them!"

She steadily backed out of my room and disappeared, returning only moments later to grab the title from the top of the stack. It was Stephen King's *It*.

"Where are you going to hide that one, Mar?"

"Under my bed where he'll never, ever look," she replied, clutching it and whispering, "I'm at the *betht* part."

I dropped her books on my desk, still upset about how she'd been treating me.

Eleanor called us downstairs. We sat on the tweed couches in the living room, listening to the pastor recommend *purifying* our bookshelves. Mom wasn't sure what he meant by that but agreed nonetheless. Hearing the edict, Marleigh turned white and looked to Dad for support, but he didn't offer any. Unless it was the sports section, Ray didn't like to read.

For the next hour, the pastor searched each room in our house, deciding what could stay and what would have to go, shelf by shelf, title by title. It wasn't technically a book burning, but it felt like it to Marleigh. She prayed he wouldn't find the cherished copy of *It* she'd hoped to finish that very night.

When the man of the cloth got to my room, Marleigh's books were piled right where I'd left them, out in the open. In one fell swoop, they went into a black garbage bag. Then the pastor placed his hand on my sister's shoulder. She trembled, more spooked by Louis than anything Stephen King had ever written.

"Is this.... all of them?" he asked me.

Marleigh shook her head, the signal for me to clam up.

"Actually, pastor," I said, knowing vengeance was mine. "There's one more. Under *her* bed," I revealed, pointing at my sister like a Salem witch.

Fearing she'd never get to finish *It*, Marleigh screamed like she'd been stabbed in the shower by Norman Bates, scurried down the hallway to her room, and slammed the door.

* * *

The following week, the pastor returned with the flock. Mom had offered him the use of our pool for baptisms but hadn't mentioned to Dad that we were the main event. He'd been accommodating with the church up to a point—but baptism? It didn't sit well with a Jew who'd walked to synagogue every Saturday since he was five.

"I don't think I can do this, Eleanor," he admitted that morning in the hallway.

But she would have none of it.

"Ray. You're getting in there, come hell or high water."

"Eleanor. Please, let's talk about this," he pleaded.

"There's nothing to talk about, Ray. Unless you want to go back to where we were before Tony, put on your trunks."

Dad bit his tongue and did as he was told.

Thirty minutes later, the pastor stood in the shallow end of our kidney-shaped pool. He submerged a few of the faithful before baptizing my mom, my sister, and me. Marleigh and I stepped out, wrapped ourselves in orange bath towels, and waited for Dad to get off his lounge chair. With my mother's prodding, he reluctantly made his way to the pool steps.

"Water's nice and warm, Ray," she said, winking as she dipped a toe in.

He turned and smiled like he had the morning they were expelled from the synagogue.

My father was six-three back then. But he wasn't just tall—he was formidable. Pastor Louis was lanky with not much stature. And here he was about to dunk Dad in the chlorine!

It was a moment of truth if I'd ever seen one.

I closely watched my father's consternated face. He'd sacrificed so much to be with our mother until that point. Mom, who was so giving yet overbearing, had gone too far this time. How could she pressure this man to jettison his faith? Dad had a choice. Accept defeat and go through with the ceremony or stand up for the first time, in a long time, for what *he* believed.

The pastor reached up, placed his hand on my father's forehead, and pressed it, trying to push him backward. But Dad wouldn't budge. So the pastor tried more forcefully, struggling to deliver him. Once again, the Jew resisted.

"No. That's it! Forget it!" Dad said, swatting the pastor's hand away. "I'm done, Louis!

He waded out of the pool, plucked a towel from Eleanor's hands, wiped his nose, and marched off past the stunned congregants.

"Ray, wait, please come back!" the pastor cried.

"I'm a Jew, Louis. A Jew!" Dad thundered as he threw open the screen door to our house.

Marleigh and I were in stitches, expecting Eleanor to be apoplectic. Yet she surprised us. She apologized to our guests, but we knew from the mist in her eyes that she'd never been so proud of Dad.

They sat on the patio that afternoon, laughing and reminiscing. And it was the last time we saw the pastor. Mom and Dad officially remarried a month later and, for a second time, vowed to stay together until death do them part.

* * *

While still God-fearing, the Moscatels began to spend more time socializing. It was the eighties, and they hosted film producers, athletes, and entertainers from all walks of life every weekend. Mom and Dad didn't have a claim to fame. But they'd worked hard to make it big, and everyone seemed to admire their moxie.

When luminaries visited Beverly Drive, they felt at ease no matter how revered they might have been in sports, showbiz, medicine, government, whatever. The atmosphere was a refreshing contrast to the pretentiousness of Beverly Hills. Our home was like the island of Rhodes before the Nazis annihilated it, filled with music, debate, and laughter. Dr. Robert had passed by then. But to Mama Rita, the liveliness under our roof was a triumphant reminder that while Hitler tried his darndest, the tyrant couldn't kill us all.

One cohort, in particular, exemplified that old Mediterranean spirit, drinking, dancing, and munching on Grandma's baklava—the novelist Rhea Kohan, Lynn Landon, and the cosmopolitan Barbara Gilbert.

Mom christened them "The A-Team" one summer's day on a chartered yacht. I'd just turned ten and was the only kid on the voyage because Eleanor had told everyone she couldn't find a sitter.

The gang was in rare form that afternoon, as was our captain, who'd gotten hammered before charting the course for Catalina. I wandered around the deck at first but, sensing the adults wanted to have their fun, stowed away in the galley, reading my favorite book, *Choose Your Own Adventure*.

Suddenly, I had a sinking sensation.

A thru-hull had ruptured, and the cabin started filling with water! I'd never been on a boat, so I wasn't sure what to do. Everybody on board was tanked, and nobody wanted to listen to a freaked-out little freckled kid clamoring to turn the ship around. But after enough hand-wringing, the captain followed me down below. Seeing the leak, he promptly ordered the vessel back to the harbor.

"Folks, we'll have to pull back into the slip," he alerted the passengers. "We've got *a little shaft* problem."

"I beg your pardon?" asked Barbara, tickled by his double entendre.

The crew steered back toward the marina, and the A-Team carried on as if nothing had happened. I sat starboard, watching my parents by the stern, embracing, in love, and completely ignoring the imminent danger.

Mom had been filming the whole trip with her clunky new camcorder. She pointed the lens at her best friend, tanning on the deck.

"Lynn, what was the best day of your life?"

"The day I met you, Eleanor," Lynn replied as she flipped over on her towel.

Mom handed the camera to Rhea and sat on Dad's lap.

"Say something, Eleanor, say something!" the novelist called out light-heartedly, zooming in on Mom.

And then, from my mother's lips, a woman who hadn't graduated college, came a stirring recital of none other than William Wordsworth.

"I wandered lonely as a cloud that floats on high o'er vales and hills, when all at once I saw a crowd, a host, of golden daffodils," she said, radiating glee.

As her companions cheered, she glanced at me lovingly and blew a kiss that sailed around the tall mast like a butterfly and landed on my cheek. And I wondered, looking into her sparkling eyes, with the harbor approaching, if it was true she couldn't find a babysitter that morning. Or if she just wanted me near her on that open sea.

* * *

My mother promised herself as a kid that she'd do everything she dreamed about once she grew up and had the means. Her big idea was to live in Paris. But she'd also fantasized about seeing the Bolshoi Ballet and swore she'd bring back real China—from China.

As a wide-eyed boy, those were faraway destinations, torn from the pages of history books, folded up like origami, and stuffed into my purple Jansport backpack like treasure maps. Waiting in the terminal, I imagined our journey would take us to museums stocked with pilfered remnants of conquered kingdoms and forbidden temples. But nothing could have prepared me for what I saw instead.

We flew Pan-Am nonstop to Hong Kong that summer. It was 1984, and the US consulate was encouraging travel excursions into the Chinese mainland to foster goodwill. One program even offered tour groups like ours a chance to see the countryside and visit orphanages. My mother, the most daring of our troupe, seized the opportunity. She arranged a day trip to a rural village outside Macau. Originally a Portuguese colony, Macau was the one city where you could gamble, the Las Vegas of Asia.

Outside its borders, the landscape told a different story.

Our transportation was a noisy yellow school bus. It barreled down a bumpy, unpaved road into a desolate wasteland toward a crimson horizon. The ride was muggy and humid, with an occasional gust of hot wind to lessen the discomfort. But Eleanor didn't vocalize any displeasure. Though she'd made it to Beverly Hills, she never once forgot her roots as a mistreated little girl in 1930s Los Angeles.

After three hours of driving in the sweltering heat, the bus pulled up ten yards from the Shenwan orphanage. It was one story, built from mud brick, with tiles missing from the roof and nothing green surrounding it. The building must have been half the length of a football field with broken awning windows and three padlocked, arched entrances at its center.

We stepped off the bus and were asked to stand close together. Two loud bells rang out, followed by a murmur. Suddenly the doors to the orphanage burst open, and throngs of brown-corduroy-clad schoolchildren came racing out. It seemed like there were waves of them. They ran toward us with liberated joy.

"*Nǐ hǎo, nǐ hǎo!*" they shouted as they approached, waving their hats and swinging their jackets above their heads like helicopter propellers.

They encircled us. Having never seen blond hair, some of the boys stroked mine like I was a rabbit in a petting zoo.

Sitting on wooden lunch tables in their mess hall that afternoon, we exchanged funny stories about California and Macau. And I quickly discovered that children are the same everywhere you go.

Mom rubbed my back as I sat next to a boy about my age.

"They're all orphans, Rafie," she explained.

"I know, Mom."

"Do you know what that means?"

"They don't have a mommy or daddy," I responded.

She kissed the side of my head and held me tight as I drank my chocolate milk. I still remember how that kiss felt. I was just like one of those Chinese kids whose blood relatives had abandoned them, but I was also *wanted*—by Eleanor and Ray. I didn't know I was adopted yet, but I was learning the real definition of family, about bonds more meaningful than the blood that ran through our veins.

* * *

That winter, we vacationed in the Soviet Union.

Our rakish guide was Marleigh's history teacher from Beverly Hills High. He advised us to pack cartons of cigarettes, Levi's, cassettes, and other Americana, which could be sold on the black market. Mom disregarded his travel tips, which proved wise because plainclothes agents shadowed us everywhere we went.

Joining us was Barbara's youngest daughter, the actress Sara Gilbert. She wasn't yet famous and still in elementary school like me. The two of us kids had never been so cold. No amount of layering seemed to protect us. When we did venture out, it was usually to museums or palaces chock-full of masterworks, most of which were created before the Bolshevik revolution.

However, the last stop on the itinerary was billed as contemporary—a visit to Vladimir Lenin's mausoleum in Moscow. The Commissar lay there embalmed in a creepy see-through casket. Eleanor and Sara thought it was grotesque, so we skipped it, planning to rendezvous with the rest of our group in Red Square, a landmark close to our hotel.

Somehow, we got lost on the way. All the buildings were nondescript, and we couldn't read or speak a lick of Russian. The few pedestrians out and about wouldn't talk to us, regardless of how distressed we became.

As night fell, the temperature dropped precipitously.

Eleanor began calling out like a madwoman, "Somebody, please help us! Somebody, please!"

Sara and I were frightened to death. For what felt like hours, we stood there shivering. There were no cell phones back then. No taxis or police to flag down. Even the agents tracking us were missing. Finally, Sara found a man willing to help. He was gaunt, with gray slacks clinging to his waist, wearing an ushanka hat and not nearly enough overcoat to keep him warm. After communicating that we needed directions, he told us what he craved in return—liquor.

In the days of the Soviet Union, alcohol wasn't sold except in limited quantities on weekends. But tourists could buy as much as they pleased and purchased it for the natives. So, Mom bought the man a fifth of Stoli, and he held up his part of the bargain, escorting us to our hotel. *It was just around the corner the whole time.*

Embarrassed yet grateful, we thanked him profusely and hurried toward the entrance.

"Proshu proshcheniya," he called as we were about to step into the revolving door.

We turned, and he pulled a book from his jacket pocket that looked like he'd been carrying around for years.

"U menya yest' koye-chto dlya tebya," he said, smiling as he ran up and handed it to us.

It was *Queen of Spades* by Alexander Pushkin. Eleanor accepted it, not understanding his motivation for gifting it. I'm not sure what the man intended by divesting what must have been one of his few possessions. Yet, I picture his face whenever I think about that frosty night in Russia.

And it reminds me of how easy it is to feel lost.

* * *

Upon returning to Beverly Hills, we learned that homes in our neighborhood had been burglarized. A month later, we became the target. Our security alarm failed, and a thug entered through a small entryway window. Hearing glass shattering downstairs, my sister Marleigh and I instinctively hid in our closets, quivering.

Eleanor wasted no time grabbing her Colt revolver. She elbowed open her bedroom door like Dirty Harry and positioned herself behind the banister.

"Whoever's down there, you listen! I have my gun here! And in three seconds, I'm coming down! I'm coming down, and I'm going to start shooting. And I'll kill you! I'll kill you!" she yelled at the top of her lungs.

Before she could start her count, our front door swung open so hard it left a hole in the drywall, and our burglar was gone. We could trace his muddy footprints through the window and back out the door.

Rarely had anybody gotten off so easy waking Eleanor up before noon.

Dad managed to sleep through the whole thing.

We never found out who did it. It could have been anybody—an ex-business partner, a jewel thief. Maybe even "the Juice."

* * *

I'm kidding. But you could never be sure with the way my family kept secrets.

The notorious OJ Simpson had begun fraternizing with Eleanor and Ray around that time while they were all being lured into a pyramid scheme for a nutritional supplement company. Since Dad was an athlete, they got along great, and like Mom, OJ's wife Nicole was vivacious, so the two couples hit it off.

Nicole eventually divorced Simpson but hadn't yet escaped his grasp by the time of her dinner with Ron Goldman on June 12th, 1994, the night she died. A part of that story has never been told, though.

Ray had been arguing with Eleanor the day earlier. He'd temporarily moved into a vacant unit in our family's Brentwood rental property, the *Casa de Rita,* across from Mezzaluna, the bistro where Nicole was dining.

Dad never cooked for himself, so he ordered takeout that evening from Mezzaluna. Walking up to the entrance, he saw Nicole waving at him through the window. Inside, she introduced him to her strapping young date. Dad had a cocktail while waiting for his order and briefly chatted with the pair. He left, thinking nothing of it.

Hours later, down the street, the couple was found murdered with Colombian neckties. My father was never questioned. And the first time he even bothered to mention the incident was in passing twenty years later as we watched a football game.

"Did I ever tell you we knew OJ and Nicole?" he said out of the blue.

"Yeah, Dad," I responded, remembering sitting on the athlete's lap at family parties.

"I saw her that night, you know."

"What do you mean *you saw her?*"

"I saw her—with that kid," he continued offhandedly.

"Uh. Did you say anything?"

"Said hello. How are you? You know, something like that."

"To the cops, Dad! Did you say anything to the cops?"

"Why would I?" he shrugged. "They never asked."

And that was the end of the conversation. Ray went back to chewing his toothpick and watching the game. It's just how our family worked.

* * *

Dad never shared his OJ story with Marleigh, either. Apart from my adoption, she was kept in the dark as much as I was.

As I entered middle school, our sibling rivalry fell by the wayside, and we grew close, bonding over the impact our father's alcoholism had on us. When she accepted a scholarship to Northwestern, I came unglued because I knew I'd be left to fend for myself with Mom and Dad. While I became the object of my parents' affection, I was as much the target of their furor. Marleigh had been a safe harbor I could run to when life was a hurricane, and now that she was gone, I missed that shelter.

Mom relied on her for emotional support when Dad's drinking worsened, a responsibility that fell to me when she left for college. It was a burden too onerous for a boy my age, but I offered Mom what hugs, kisses, and empathy I could, knowing the hell Dad's drinking caused. Mom drank too, but Ray had a more serious issue and wasn't always there in the ways a husband should be. So, I was brought in sometimes as a substitute companion, a position for which I was woefully unqualified.

Tagging alongside Mom made me feel like the protagonist in John Cheever's *The Swimmer*, an underdressed guest bouncing from party to party, never being invited or getting anywhere. Mom, on the other hand, was a VIP. My father was, aesthetically, her ideal partner, an ex-jock and doctor who knew how to throw back a drink and tell a joke.

For a while, I didn't know how I fit into their rags-to-riches story.

Mom and Dad were older when they adopted me. My schoolmates' parents were much younger and hipper by comparison. They'd lived through the sixties and seen Jimi Hendrix at the Palladium. My parents? They survived the Depression and saw Nat King Cole at The Cocoanut Grove. Their parents were up-and-comers. Mine could have been grandparents. For a time, I considered the age gap a hex. I saw my mother as the biblical Sarah and my father as Abraham. To confuse matters, they had good genes and better plastic surgeons. They didn't seem to age. It was like living with two pictures of Dorian Gray.

Most of my classmates' parents were intimidated by Eleanor and didn't even attempt to get to know Dad. So, the kids I hung around with were often sons and daughters of live-in maids or, in some cases, offspring of wealthy old fathers and nubile mothers. One was Pia Zadora, a dainty Polish actress who'd married corporate raider Meshulam Riklis when she was twenty-three, and he was mid-century. He wasted considerable personal finances trying to get her fledgling career off the ground—a drop in the bucket for the Israeli businessman who'd developed high-yield junk bonds.

We met the Riklis family through a realtor friend who'd just sold them Pickfair, the estate built by Douglas Fairbanks and Mary Pickford. Ignoring the concerns of preservationists, Pia had razed the historical residence, citing ghosts. Scotty and I overheard her discuss the controversy at her second house on Summit Ridge. I was eleven and agitated because we were both stuck there at a *Little Mermaid*-themed birthday for her daughter.

Pia was kind of like us, an orphan. As a child actor, her youth had been stolen, and I think the woman saw a little piece of herself in Scotty. She treated him like her own son, inviting him everywhere. It's probably why he didn't complain as much as I did in her company. He walked around her house as if he lived there.

"Bucky. Come here," Scotty whispered, waving me over to a flagstone path leading to her tennis court.

I followed him around the bend while he checked to see if it was safe to light a cigarette.

"Here, take this," he said, handing me a menthol.

Having never smoked, I hacked after inhaling. The taste was bitter, a flavor marking the twilight of my childhood.

"Are you okay?" Scotty asked.

"Yeah," I lied as I passed it to him.

I rinsed my hands in a granite fountain on the way back, hoping to wash away the odor, and dried them on my pants. I knew I'd done something wrong and felt rebellious.

But nobody even noticed I was gone.

The remainder of that day was spent by the front door, hoping to leave. But Mom was having too much fun and never departed before the cake was served. I rejoiced when she finally told me to ask the valet to pull her car around.

As I handed in the ticket, I saw my favorite Laker, Earvin "Magic" Johnson standing across the street outside his house. Scotty was next to me, and we began waving like idiots. We couldn't believe it when he started smiling and waving back. But it was too good to be true—he'd recognized Scotty's dad, the Donald, looming behind us like Dracula.

"Hey there, Earvin!" Don said.

"How's the party?" Magic replied.

"Not bad. When are you gonna come play for me?"

"You don't have that kinda money," the Hall-of-Famer laughed.

Uncle Don mumbled something under his breath. Scotty and I could tell he wasn't happy with the exchange, and we kept our mouths shut.

* * *

When December rolled around, Mom and I headed over Coldwater Canyon to Barbara's Christmas party. She was the daughter of Harry Crane, a golden age of Hollywood screenwriter who wrote *The Honeymooners*. I was warned never to disrupt the poker game he hosted for his friends during that event. They all looked alike to me, and I'd stare at that round table, watching them smoke their big cigars, listen to them crack dirty jokes, and age. It got smaller each year until nobody was left to shuffle the deck.

Barbara's oldest daughter, Melissa, would float in about a third through the night. She was glamorous and adopted, like me. Mom was "Auntie Ellie" to her and, like much of America, had watched her grow up playing Laura Ingalls on *Little House on the Prairie*. The first time

I remember being there was fourteen years after my brother's death. Each time I saw Melissa, I knew she thought of him. She was on set the night of his accident.

"Rafael *Albert*. I loved your brother," she'd say, bending down and kissing me on the cheek before sending me down to see her little sister Sara.

I walked down that hallway alone, hearing the adult laughter fade behind me and the ruckus coming from Sara's room. It was like the set of *The Toy*, the size of a living room, with a sitting area and every amusement imaginable. When it came to her mother's parties, though, Sara was a recluse, forced to put up with kids like me relegated to her bedroom while their parents hobnobbed. She lay on her bed reading and hardly spoke, treating me like a leper. It was unpleasant, feeling unwelcome every year at Christmastime.

Our mothers routinely partnered us up. But no matter where we went together, I felt invisible to Sara, whether at a Christmas party or lost on a cold street in Russia. She wasn't cruel, but she never let her guard down. On the rare occasion that she'd invite me somewhere, it was always at her thoughtful mother's behest.

When I was twelve, Sara was tasked with keeping her eye on me at Mountain Meadow Ranch, a summer camp outside Reno, Nevada. I would've been happy had she treated me like a pesky little brother, but she barely acknowledged my existence throughout the years we camped there. When she did say hello, it was with a boyfriend who relentlessly mocked me. I shouldn't have taken it personally, but I was young and malleable. Nobody had ever made me feel so small by saying so little.

I never understood why she was so aloof. I'd like to believe she kept her distance because she knew the secret of my adoption, and hiding things from others made her uneasy.

* * *

Nevertheless, Mountain Meadow was the best thing to happen to a boy who'd only known city life. I spent most summers on that ranch fishing and horseback riding. But it was designed to instill a work ethic, too. At the end of each day, they had me feed their pigs, trudging a quarter mile up a dirt hill with buckets of slop from the commissary to dump in metal troughs outside the barn. It was a dirty job, and I loved it.

I was also hitting puberty and unaware that my past was subconsciously gnawing at me. It manifested in repugnant behavior, lasting almost until I learned I was given up for adoption. Establishing healthy, platonic relationships with girls felt impossible. In hindsight, I realize those difficulties originated from profound abandonment and trust issues.

Rejection often precipitated my misogyny—initially at that summer camp by a country girl named Heather who'd taught me to ride an English saddle in the horse ring. I still recall how her jet-black hair blew in the wind as she rounded the barrels. She was my first crush. I'd lie awake each night, looking out my window toward her cabin, thinking about what she might be doing.

It took every last ounce of courage to approach her at the dance on the last night of camp.

"Heather," I said, my voice cracking.

"Your zipper," she replied, noticing I'd left my barn door open.

"Oh, thanks," I responded and foolhardily continued, "Do you—"

But she shook her head and walked away. *As if we'd never met.*

I imploded.

Had she said no, or at least let me finish, her refusal may have been easier to stomach. But she just left me standing there with tears welling. I took revenge by shouting obscenities at her as we hiked back to our cabins—words that should never come from any child's mouth.

"Everyone knows you're a dumb slut, Heather!" I growled like a dog.

Worse, I persuaded other boys to join in the brutish chants which echoed across the meadow. It was too late to be sent home, but I'd never be invited back. My parents were rightly disgusted with my behavior. I was acting out and so sad. I didn't know how else to ask for help. It was the beginning of an inkling that a monster was hiding inside me. Had I known earlier of my adoption, it may have been unmasked. But I remained a lost boy and later a bewildered young man imprisoned by that old lie.

* * *

When I returned from camp, Eleanor had decided that what would help us all was a change of scenery. She'd started packing our bags. A few days later, I was at the airport with a fourteen-inch steamer trunk filled to the brim with school clothes, bedsheets, and toiletries. Mom and Marleigh were headed to Paris, and I was being sent to a Swiss boarding school. Dad would come along to help us settle in.

I lagged behind, dragging my feet and hoping we'd miss our plane. Suddenly my eyes lit up like a death row inmate granted a pardon. I saw giants ahead, traversing the glossy white floor of the Tom Bradley terminal, adorned in gold and purple attire. They moved silently like a family of brontosaurs, the smaller creatures among us gazing up at their long swinging limbs as they passed. It was our hometown heroes, the Los Angeles Lakers! Magic Johnson led the pack, with Kareem Abdul-Jabbar bringing up the rear.

I knocked over my trunk and bolted toward them.

"Rafie! Get back here," yelled my father.

"You're Kareem!" I said as I ran beside the all-star center.

He didn't stop moving but looked down at me from what felt like high up in the clouds.

"Smart kid," he teased Ray, who'd caught up to me, put his hand on my shoulders, and held me back.

I was starstruck. My sister stood at a distance, unimpressed.

"Did you hear that?" I asked, turning to Marleigh. "Did you hear what he said?"

"Yup. It's called sarcasm. Look it up in the dictionary."

I didn't have time to. Eleanor was on the opposite end of the terminal, expecting us to catch up.

"Mom, it's the Lakers! The Lakers! They're world champions!" I declared.

"I don't care who they are," she replied as we hustled to the gate. "They're not going to make us miss this flight."

* * *

All my intrepid mother asked of me that ripening autumn was that I not *completely* ruin her Paris vacation. Mom had dreamed about the trip for years. She'd rented a flat on Boulevard Raspail across from a former Prime Minister and made a list of a million things she wanted to do, like learning French.

Marleigh was doing a semester at the Sorbonne. And to keep me out of her hair, Mom enrolled me for the fall at The American School In Switzerland. It was nestled in a hill town on the northern side of Lago di Lugano, equidistant from France, Italy, Germany, and Austria. I was to study there rigorously alongside presumably more disciplined children of textile magnates, executives, and royal families.

Eleanor checked her watch as I sat hunched over on my big steamer trunk in the dormitory. She couldn't wait to get out of there. Dad wasn't too broken up about leaving, either. I'd been a pain in their necks lately, irritated by raging hormones and doleful from steadily worsening acne.

"You'll be fine, Rafie," Marleigh said, comforting me.

"I guess," I replied, leaning into her shoulder.

"Do what they tell you, kid," my dad warned, adjusting the newsboy on his bald head.

I watched from the balcony as Ray squeezed in behind the wheel of the candy-red Peugeot Mom had rented for the drive to Paris. She rolled down her window and looked up at me, having said nothing the entire time.

"Enjoy," she mouthed as they sped off.

It wasn't a suggestion. It was a threat. One you might receive with a dead fish wrapped in the local paper. They would be one country away. But it felt like they'd flown back to the States or been shot from a canon. And I was, for the first time, entirely alone, a stranger in a strange land. I hadn't even met the headmaster. I'd spent five minutes with a dorm chaperone before my folks left and didn't know when classes would be held or how to find the bathroom. I held my pimpled face in my sweaty palms and closed my eyes.

That's when Zeki, an ostentatious young Turk, walked in.

"What are you moping about, dickface?" he asked, chewing bubble gum as he listened to his Walkman and checked the room out.

"Sorry, what?" I said, startled.

He was about my height, with brown bangs sweeping over his egg-shaped head.

"I'm taking the top bunk, bitch," he stated, dropping his trunk and vaulting onto the mattress above me.

Zeki was the only child of an airline executive and an heiress, and a blast to be around. Along with another roommate, Julian, a Swiss native, we became like the three musketeers. Our camaraderie lifted my spirits. And because Julian was already six feet tall, we looked older by simply being around him—which helped us take advantage of Europe's already lax drinking laws.

I was growing up way too fast.

Usually, after curfew, we'd sneak out to a bus stop, bribe the driver not to report us, and hide under the seats like a pack of rats until our bus reached the disco. That debauchery continued for weeks until I got so bombed one night that I tried to sock an upperclassman. My jab didn't land but infuriated him and I was lucky not to have lost my buck teeth in the altercation. Soon, stories of our escapades spread around junior high, and our plans were foiled.

Early the next morning I was summoned to the headmaster's office. My accomplice's parents were alumni and big donors, so they were let off the hook. But I was *permanently suspended* and told to pack my things. *Nobody was ever expelled from The American School In Switzerland because it would sully its stellar reputation.*

As the headmaster droned about my future, I watched the wind rustle the spruce trees outside the crystal diamond windows behind him, and it began snowing. Winter had begun, and soon I'd answer to a higher authority in my life—my mother.

* * *

At daybreak, my dorm chaperones put me on a train departing for Paris. I noticed my luggage hadn't been loaded and jumped onto the icy platform.

"What about my trunk?" I asked.

"We'll send it," they bluntly responded as they walked towards me.

I took the hint and hopped back onto the train.

I was off to face Eleanor, and so feared her retribution that I envisaged leaping from the caboose as it crossed one of the suspension bridges along the route. But as the conductor came through to punch tickets, I knew it was futile to try and run. It was time to pay the piper. I slumped against the window and fell asleep.

My train shot through a long tunnel in the Swiss Alps, and when I awoke, the snow on the windows had melted. We pulled into the Gare de Lyon train station nine hours later. I hopped off and stared around the colossal Belle Époque structure from the concourse. And as I admired the architecture, there waiting was my sister Marleigh, stylishly dressed with a beret and giving me a slow clap.

"Mom. Is. Going. To. Kill you," she said.

"I know," I replied, jittery.

"No, I mean, you are literally going to die. Today. A few minutes from now."

I believed my comeuppance would be severe, *but at least it wouldn't leave a mark,* I told myself. I'd been spanked as a child and was too old for corporal punishment. My mistake this time was costly, however. It wasn't just the squandered boarding school tuition but the time Eleanor would waste dealing with me, a delinquent. I dreaded her.

Our taxi dropped us a short walk from Mom's apartment.

"Watch out for the dogshit," my sister warned me as she walked ahead.

But I was too distracted by thoughts of impending doom and slipped mightily on a fresh dropping of sidewalk poop.

"Ahh! Fuck!" I yelled as I lay there, Parisians passing by expressing little sympathy.

Marleigh ran back to check on me, but when she realized I was fine almost busted her gut, kneeling to catch her breath. She helped me up, and we made our way to the apartment.

I smelled like a porta potty as we stepped into the ironclad, claustrophobic lift at Mom's place. Five flights up, my sister opened the cage door to the suite, and I followed her. I stood in awe at the entry, marveling at the wainscotting, crown molding, chandeliers, and fainting couches.

What had I done? It was Eleanor's lifelong dream to live in Paris. How could I have been so selfish to have ruined it? Marleigh showed me to a bedroom with a terrace, and I watched a crane hoist oversized furniture into a neighboring flat. A cool current of air tickled the nape of my neck as the door opened, and Mom walked in. She sat on the daybed, sighing. I turned and ran to her, begging for forgiveness. Her arm closed around me like an elephant's trunk.

"Take a shower. I'll wash your clothes, and we'll talk later," Mom instructed, kissing my temple and crossing into an adjoining room.

Rather than send me back to Los Angeles, *she gave me a key.* One I would guard like the Holy Grail. To pass the time I wasn't in school, I spent afternoons wandering around the Louvre and picking up shopping orders for her at the Bon Marché. There were bookstores everywhere, many with titles in English. I began collecting biographies and memoirs, imagining I might sit down and write my own one day.

Now that I'm a parent, some thirty years later, I've learned that sometimes when you spare the rod, metaphorically at least, you risk spoiling the child. But Eleanor also taught me that you've got to let kids make their own mistakes. That's the best informal education I received that fall—the year I fucked up my life, *excusez mon français.*

* * *

Mom's lease expired, and we came home to the devastating news that Michael Landon had pancreatic cancer and was given months to live. My folks hadn't talked to him in ages, but he'd arranged for old friends to visit and say their last goodbyes.

Mom stayed back, but I went with Dad. I was fourteen, and it had been eight years since we'd last seen him. Michael was sitting in an armchair, his hands resting on his jeans. Though his days were numbered, and he was pensive, he didn't look as frightened as I'd pictured someone in his position might be.

"Hey, Bucky," he said, less energetic than when he'd first named me.

I approached him inchmeal, not knowing whether to hug the man or shake his hand. He reached out, and I gently embraced him before stepping back behind my father.

"Hello, Raymond," Michael said, smiling at his old best friend.

Ray stood there, unable to speak. One of the Landons came over and ushered me away so the two pals could visit. Then Dad took a chair and muttered something that made Michael laugh, but he struggled with what to say next.

"I'm sorry, Mike," he said, glancing around the room and holding back his deepest emotions, just as he'd been trained to as a boy.

"It's okay, Raymond. I've lived a good life," Michael replied solemnly.

I watched from a distance as they sat there quietly, having shared some of the best years of their lives, with no words left to say to one another.

Journeys

In September, I enrolled at Beverly Hills High—the same year *90210* debuted on television. The primetime soap was popular among my classmates, but I felt embarrassed by its outlandish depiction of our formative years. Our house was once home to the show's creator Aaron Spelling. He vacated it after divorcing *Morticia Addams,* who then sold it to Eleanor.

Spelling had a knack for spinning gold from dull yarns. He knew his audience wanted to escape from the daily grind and journey far from home. *90210* served up that fantasy. It was a formulaic, non-contextualized diorama of opulence. But unlike Spelling's melodrama, there were no extravagant perks at the real Beverly High, like Perrier in the water fountains or valet parking. Kids had flashy cars, but not me. I drove Ray's used sedan, an '84 sunburnt Cadillac with torn leather seats, dented bumpers, and a hundred thousand miles on it.

I felt out of place from day one, like a foreign exchange student, partly because of a pronounced red rash beneath my nose. To look older in Europe, Zeki and Julian unwisely recommended I shave before my beard came in. The blade stunted the growth of skin on my upper lip, which remained discolored for years. So, on top of a typical teenager's complexion, I started ninth grade looking like Pedro from *Napoleon Dynamite.*

Luckily, I found a welcome wagon in the school's drama department. Marleigh had starred in their plays, and teachers remembered her fondly. And at Beverly, drama nerds weren't ostracized. We were in the entertainment capital of the world, after all.

For a while, I thrived. As a sophomore, I tried out for *Oliver!*, ending up in the chorus as one of Fagin's orphans. On opening night, as I nervously crouched beneath a set piece, a castmate pointed out a distinguished gentleman with silver tips and a chiseled face in the front row of the audience. He'd passed out snoring, and we couldn't help but crack up. But when the curtain came down, a stagehand snapped at us for laughing at her uncle—Frank Sinatra.

I confessed my embarrassment to Dad as soon as I came home. And to make me feel better, he told me how he'd once run into the singer in the john. But while he could sense something else was bothering me, he didn't probe much further. Dad loved me, but I don't think he ever really knew how to reach me.

* * *

The closing night of that coming-of-age musical would be my final performance as an actor. It had nothing to do with insulting Sinatra, though. My acne had flared up and become so distracting that classmates couldn't concentrate on their lines while rehearsing. My parents and sisters were the only ones who could look at my face without losing their train of thought. Eleanor took me to see the city's best dermatologists.

Nobody could help.

Shunned by my peers, I roamed the empty halls of school during lunch each day, pretending I was on my way somewhere or late for something. Yet I had nowhere to go and no one to talk to. Scotty had been placed in a different school, and we'd drifted apart.

After class, one afternoon, the drama teacher Ms. Evans, a dilettante unsuited to be any kind of educator, took me aside.

"Rafie. How do I say this nicely? Your pimples, honey. I was in the balcony section today and could see them up there. Hasn't your mother tried to take you to see a doctor?"

"Yes, I told her," for the hundredth time.

But she was right. My face was a minefield—every inch covered in pustules. And while blaming me for something beyond my control was outrageous, I was too self-conscious to defend myself. Deflated, I never stepped onto a stage again.

All I could do was walk those halls alone, wallowing in my gloom, until the school bell freed me. Like Mom and Michael Landon, I ran home, taking refuge from the ridicule behind the steam of hot showers and reading through biographies I'd brought back from Paris.

It wasn't my fault I was revolting. Still, I believed I deserved to be unsightly for my sins—smoking with Scotty, drinking in school, cussing at women, and disobeying authority. Cystic acne was my prison sentence for being rotten to the core. And I convinced myself that God had molded me into an introvert for my own good.

By the onset of junior year, my face had gotten worse. Friends hadn't come around, and I grew despondent. I began to think life would be better if I just took my mom's revolver and killed myself.

Then a little miracle happened.

I was reacquainted with Kris, the castmate with whom I'd poked fun at Frank Sinatra. I'd been wandering the halls when I found him with his back against a locker, wearing a long-sleeved flannel and doodling in his notepad.

"What's up?" he asked, his blond bangs covering his face like the crest of a wave.

"Hi," I said, delighted somebody was talking to me.

"It's Kris. From drama. We were in *Oliver!* together, remember?"

"Yeah, I know," I replied, warming up.

Kris saw my ugly mug, smiled, and continued drawing. He was the first kid who'd spoken to me socially in forever. I wondered if he'd heard what people were saying about me. Their comments were so tormenting that I'd cordoned myself off, like a condemned building awaiting demolition. But Kris didn't seem to give a damn. We sat together that afternoon, chatting until lunch was over.

My new friend was an accomplished child actor. He despised the profession, but his mother had dragged him to auditions from infancy, and casting agents loved him. Kris was still in demand when we met, doing Dr. Pepper commercials and playing the character Lonnie on *Roseanne*, alongside Sara Gilbert, in the role of Darlene. He said she'd also given him the cold shoulder and not to take it personally.

Though he'd been the breadwinner for most of his life, his family treated him like a workhorse. He lived with his alcoholic mother in a moldy one-bedroom she never cleaned. Having long divorced his father, a liquor store delivery man, her motherhood was spent sponging off Kris. She'd robbed him of many things, foremost his education.

That's one reason he was hanging out in the halls. He didn't have time to develop friendships because he was always on the clock. As we bonded, he opened up about his battle with scoliosis and why he never took his shirt off in gym class. The disease would contribute to his drinking and lead him down the same spiral as his mother. And as his body changed and he grew stubble, work began drying up. Soon they would be thinking of replacing him on *Roseanne*.

In the meantime, we'd be there for one another and need that support because the following semester, we'd take biology with the most feared teacher in the history of Beverly Hills High.

* * *

Mr. Hale was menacing—a carbon copy of boxer Muhammad Ali, with beefy forearms, scarred knuckles, and a perfectly cut Afro. Even his chubby cheeks looked mean. He sat the entire lecture, staring at us like plebs. We were terrified of this man.

"Open y'books," he'd say in his baritone, snorting as class began.

He never told us what page—just *open y'books*.

Licking his chops, he'd continue, "Okay. Photosynthesis..."

It was monotonous, bell to bell. Only fear kept us from falling asleep. The best and brightest, including my sister, flunked. But neither Kris nor I could stand the thought of summer school. After class one day, we decided to approach the stoic figure.

"Mr. Hale?" I asked, swallowing my words.

He turned around like a medieval hangman, a small gold cross around his neck.

"What do you boys want?" he asked, tapping his fat fingers on a Bunsen burner.

"Uh. Mr. Hale. Uh. We were wondering—"

"Wondering what, boy?" he roared, his walnut eyes widening. "Spit it out!"

"If there's something we can do. To get a better grade," said Kris.

Mr. Hale leaned against a lab bench and stared at us for a few minutes.

"Tutoring. Every Thursday. Lunchtime," he said, expressionless.

Nodding, we backed out of the classroom like we'd stared down a grizzly.

Yet we showed up each week and broke bread with that surprisingly magnanimous man—the only two kids that year to take him up on the offer. He made us laugh and took a genuine interest in our future. And we learned!

But when the final came, he proctored like a corrections officer. Nobody dared to cheat. Everybody finished early, including the valedictorian, who threw his arms up and shook his head as if a great injustice had occurred.

"Since we're all done, how about we grade these?" Mr. Hale asked, waving the tests in the air and looking at Kris and me. "Boys, go on up and put these things through the scantron machine."

He handed us the tests and answer key, and we dashed into the stairwell to the second-floor teacher's lounge, where they kept the computer.

Halfway up, Kris grabbed my shirt.

"Wait, Rafie. Mr. Hale's trying to tell us something," he said, a devious look in his eyes.

It made me skittish that he was proposing we cheat. But I wanted it to make sense. We'd built a rapport with Mr. Hale, and he liked us. And I'd never gotten a better grade than Marleigh. We sat on the steps and agreed to *update* our answers.

"Try to miss some, so it isn't obvious," Kris suggested, hurriedly filling in the ovals.

"Okay," I replied, ensuring a few were incorrect.

We ran the tests through the machine, returned to class, and tried to slip away.

"Hold on there, boys. Hold on," Mr. Hale said. "Let's see how everybody did."

Kris and I gulped as he began reading the results. They were worse than we expected—even the valedictorian barely passed. Finally, he came to our names. Our scores were ninety-six and ninety-two, respectively. The class erupted, knowing something was awry. But Mr. Hale shut them down by slamming his fist on the table.

He removed his glasses, rubbed his eyes for an eternity, and said, "Boys. I'm gonna ask you this one time. You have anything to tell me?"

Kris and I turned to each other, guilty as all hell.

* * *

The next day Mr. Hale let the class go early but held me back.

"Rafee-el."

As he scribbled in his grade book, I shuffled towards him in my oversized hoodie.

"Where's your little friend?"

Kris hadn't shown up. Neither had several kids that day.

"I'm not sure, Mr. Hale," I answered truthfully.

"What y'all did yesterday, proud of it?"

My stomach sank. Not because I thought he might fail me but because I'd betrayed his trust. He lowered his reading glasses and addressed me like a son.

"Been teaching this class for over twenty-five years," he stated, pinching the bridge of his nose.

"I'm sorry, Mr. Hale."

"No, nope. Don't apologize," he said, pointing at me. "You're not the first. Not the last. But what you need to learn here, and I'll tell your little buddy this too, is this—anyone can spend life lying—all of it. Might even get away with it. Might even get away with lying to me. Never happened yet. But that doesn't matter because you'll never be able to lie to yourself."

He wasn't just right.

He was the greatest teacher I ever had.

I retook the exam at lunch and scored a B+. He dropped it to a D, a penalty for my academic dishonesty. I wouldn't see the man much after that, but his words would stick with me. At the time, though, his mercy and wisdom weren't enough to get me on the straight and narrow. I was incorrigible.

Yet I felt lucky to be alive after running into Kris the next day. He was wearing his flannel, his hair was disheveled, and he'd been crying.

* * *

We shared a meatball sandwich at lunch, and he told me what had happened two nights earlier. A classmate he'd known since kindergarten had been riding his mountain bike up in the canyons a few blocks from my house when a vehicle struck him. He was taken to the emergency room and succumbed to his injuries within hours.

The boy was seventeen, like my brother Albert.

After school, I shared news of his passing with Mom as she fixed a wig in her vanity. She became still when I uttered the boy's name, *Elione*. Setting down her comb, she covered her lips. Then, harkening back to the time "she was pregnant with me," she recalled a foreboding exchange she'd once had with an expectant mother.

The woman had been strolling past our house one afternoon and was intrigued by the sight of Mom's Rolls-Royce. She glared at it, polished and poised like an exotic animal, asleep on our new brick driveway. The clean blue California license plate, ELIONE, glimmered in the sunlight, calling to her.

Somebody had left the front gate open, so the woman stepped up to our porch, knocked on the door, and Mom answered.

"Hello. I'm sorry. I don't mean to be a bother, but—"

"It's no bother, dear. How can I help you?"

"Your car," said the woman, gesturing toward the Rolls. "It's majestic."

"Thank you," Mom replied.

"I hope I'm not imposing, but what's it mean? The plate, Elione?" she asked, besotted with the vehicle.

"Oh. It's kind of after my name, Eleanor."

"I like it very much," she remarked, soothing her belly.

The woman left, and Mom, still in a fog over Albert, hadn't thought about the incident since. Their connection was diabolical, though—two mothers whose precious sons had died the same way, at the same age, tethered by that chance encounter.

That day was tailor-made for Eleanor to tell me everything about where I came from. *She didn't.* Yet no matter how great her deception, I'm still here to tell you about it. And living in the dark, even for thirty years, is nothing compared to what those boys lost.

I was the lucky one.

* * *

Kris was never as fortunate, either.

Toward the end of junior year, he was expelled for bringing a prop gun to school *at the drama teacher's request.* When confronted by the principal, Ms. Evans cowered and threw him under the bus. Police arrested and made an example of him—the gun charge trumped up because of recent school shootings. He was sent to a crummy one-room building for exiled students at the edge of campus. But Kris's social standing, or lack thereof, made it easy for the administration to throw the book at him. His mother tried to advocate for her son, but her disorganized pleas hurt his case. And much like my Swiss boarding school, Beverly High had a double standard of its own.

A week before his expulsion hearing, I was sitting on the steps outside French class when a boy named Mort Sahl, Jr. pulled out two *real* guns from his backpack. He'd stolen them from his father, a well-known comedian and satirist. Mort was a fellow hall wanderer, but we weren't close friends. Though we were both shy, cerebral, and decidedly out of place at Beverly, Kris had warned me that he was too far out, even for a misfit like me. But while his guns were a red flag, I didn't report him. Everything happened so fast that I couldn't process it.

"Where did you get those?" I inquired.

"They're my dad's," he admitted. "Told me I could borrow them."

I couldn't tell if he was serious or inherited his sense of humor from his father.

"What are you going to do with them?" I asked, alarmed.

"Not sure yet," he said, grinning at me. "What do you think I should do?"

"Keep 'em in there," I replied, trying to act cool.

He described their mechanics in detail, brandishing the firearms like collector's items. As the first bell rang and students began to arrive, he tucked the weapons into his bag. I followed him into the classroom, shaken by what I'd seen, but it never crossed my mind what might happen next.

Our teacher, Madame Kinneman, didn't either.

Madame was a time capsule. She could have been an extra in *Hairspray* or played a rigid proctor in Pink Floyd's *Another Brick in the Wall*. A staunch disciplinarian, she'd have slapped you on the knuckles with a ruler if she could get away with it, but boy, could she teach. Those educators, to me, were the finest—strict yet benevolent when it mattered. Her cheeks were layered in powder, so much so that when she stood on her toes to write on the chalkboard, you couldn't tell if it was chalk dust or makeup falling off her face. She wore a pungent perfume that could have been a home concoction. And when Madame smiled, which was seldom, there was an impressive gap between her front teeth.

She avoided eye contact and lectured with her back to the class. I kept my sights on Mort because of what he'd shown me minutes before. But when I shifted focus momentarily to find my place in the textbook, a collective gasp sucked the air out of the room.

There was Mort. Standing beside his desk and pointing his gun at the back of Madame's head. We were paralyzed with fear—even the jocks.

"What is all the commotion back there?" Madame asked, cluelessly jotting down the day's lesson on conjugating verbs. "*Je suis, tu es, il est, nous sommes, vous êtes, ils sont.*"

My classmates looked at one another, mortified. Yet, I was less afraid because of the baffling way Madame handled the situation. Not once did she turn around.

"For heaven's sake. What is going on?" she asked again.

"I'm pointing a gun at you, Madame," Mort said, still aiming at her.

"A *gun*, monsieur?" she paused. "Do you mean *pistolet?*"

"Yes, Madame," Mort answered.

It was as if we were watching Bud Cort's tour de force in *Harold and Maude*. The gun could have gone off at any moment.

"What is the *pistolet* for, monsieur?" Madame asked.

"To kill you, Madame," he responded.

She set the chalk down and sighed.

"Monsieur Sahl. Do us *all* a favor and sit down this instant. We've wasted too much time," she vented, resuming her lesson plan.

Inexplicably, he sat down and hid the gun in his backpack. Why? I never understood. Maybe he was starving for attention, something he might not have gotten enough of at home. But thank heavens.

At the end of that day, I sat with him on the school steps and watched as his dad picked him up in a red Ferrari. Mort got in and gave me a thumbs-up.

"See you tomorrow, Raf," he said as the pistons fired and the roadster took off.

Despite a class full of witnesses, he faced no consequences. Mort died two years later, more or less the way Scotty did.

I've watched that tragic scene up close too many times—troubled young outcasts like me whose fates were sealed by loving yet misguided parents. Draping over the mirrors reflecting the turmoil within their children's souls made them undoubtedly more vulnerable to their monsters.

* * *

In my senior year, the monster in me found itself caged—temporarily.

Not having Kris around at school had left me depressed and lacking real friends again. Too embarrassed to admit that to my parents, I came up with fake names whenever I was asked whom I'd had lunch or was spending my time with.

One Saturday night, I made a big mistake with Eleanor after taking the Cadillac without permission. Kris was sick at home, and I had nowhere to go, so I drove around the hills aimlessly. When I pulled into our driveway around midnight, Mom was waiting up, furious.

"God damn it!" she screamed, breaking away from my father and marching down the porch steps toward the car like she was going to hit me.

I got out and tried to walk past her, but she gripped my collar and dragged me toward the front door.

"Get in that fucking house!" she yelled.

I could tell she'd been drinking.

"Where were you?" questioned my father, standing at her side.

"Out with my friends," I stated as fact.

"With Kris?" Mom asked, not fond of him.

"No. Just some people you don't know."

"You liar," she said, walking out of the room.

I sat there crying as my father followed her to the den. Then, enraged, I bounded upstairs toward my room but stopped at the landing when I saw Eleanor's bedroom door open. I knew she kept her revolver there, and it crossed my mind to take it. I wasn't sure what I'd do with it, whether to shoot myself, them, or all of us, but I was foaming and made my way in.

She usually left her gun by the nightstand when she went to sleep, so I looked for it there, but it was missing. I got on my knees to check under the bed. Suddenly I heard the sound of footsteps coming up the stairs and ran out.

"Why are you in there? Why are you in my room!" Mom said angrily, catching me as I came out her door.

I didn't give her an answer, and our fight continued for hours. At around three in the morning, I threatened to kill myself.

"Go ahead," Mom said, baiting me.

"Fine," I replied, storming into my room and kicking open the door to my balcony.

I climbed over the railing and leaned back dramatically above the front yard.

"Rafie! Don't be a fool! Get back in here," said Dad from out an adjacent window.

I shook my head, closed my eyes, and let go—falling fewer than nine feet onto a boxwood hedge. The next morning, I woke up with a sore ass and a broken finger.

* * *

Not only was I in trouble for acting like an imbecilic teenager, but Mom had received a call from my career counselor. He warned her about my grades and said I'd need spectacular SATs to get into any university. She'd planned to discuss it with me when she discovered her car missing.

My folks went to great lengths to get me in line. I was grounded indefinitely, drug tested each week, and had my driving privileges suspended. Going forward, Lynn's son, Christopher, would drive me to school in the mornings, an errand he begrudgingly accepted. I'd ride public transportation home after school, transferring at the Santa Monica and Cañon Drive stop and wait there an hour for the next bus. When I got tired, I'd sit on the curb watching cars.

Most of the time, I read.

Ever since Oliver Stone's film, *The Doors,* had been released, I'd been a super fan, collecting every biopic I could find on the band. That afternoon I was devouring one on Jim Morrison, *The Lizard King,* when an older guy, all in black, began talking to me.

"Great songwriter," he remarked, noticing my book jacket.

"Yeah," I agreed.

He impressed me, reciting the lyrics to *Ghost Song* as if he'd written them.

"A vast radiant beach and cooled jeweled moon. Couples naked race down by its quiet side. And we laugh like soft, mad children."

Wow, I thought. *This guy knows his stuff.*

I was enlivened and said I'd dreamed of becoming a writer.

He then digressed, sharing flashbacks from his unfettered youth—salacious, risqué experiences that made me feel like I'd been raised in a monastery. A meticulous storyteller, he said he'd published a novel all about it in the eighties. He was surprised I didn't recognize the title, considering how voracious a reader I said I was.

When our bus pulled up, I threw my backpack on and boarded with my monthly pass. He bought a transfer and passed me on the way to the back. I watched as he rested his Doc Martens on the seat beside him and sat lengthwise, looking sapped. I couldn't tell if he'd lied to me for the past hour or how reliable a narrator he was. But when we reached my stop, he called out my name as I hopped off.

"Good luck with the writing, Rafael," the goth said.

"Thanks. I'll read your book. What did you say the name of it was?"

"*Less Than Zero,*" he answered, tipping his Ray-Bans.

I called Marleigh when I got home, and she clued me in that I'd just met Bret Easton Ellis. Or some random posing as him. But she didn't care about that. She wanted to know how well my new acne medicine, Accutane, was working. I reported that it was a miracle drug, and though I'd be left with a few scars, the worst of it was over.

Mom then interrupted our conversation to announce that a letter had come. Having been rejected from every school, I didn't get my hopes up. But I'd worked hard to score high on my entrance exams, and this envelope was fatter than the rest. I about lost my mind when I learned I'd been accepted to the University of California.

* * *

While happy for me, Eleanor had one condition I'd need to meet before attending college. Since losing Mama Rita that year, she'd started retracing her Sephardic lineage and become involved with the synagogue. They were raising money for a birthright trip to Israel, and she'd reserved a ticket for me, hoping I might reconnect with God before leaving home.

Spiritually, I was lost as the Hebrews who'd wandered in that hot desert for forty years, and I didn't want to go. But Mom wouldn't negotiate. Realizing I had no choice, I signed up without reading the itinerary.

On our way to the Middle East, we stopped in Rome to visit the Vatican, which felt like skipping ahead to *The New Testament* before getting the backstory in *The Holy Scriptures*. I was buddied up with a diminutive, ill-mannered boy with a twang from the Carolinas named Richie, who pestered everybody. Not ten minutes into the tour of the Sistine Chapel, he'd violated their rules against flash photography. Since I was standing close to him, we were both detained, booted, and ordered to wait outside at a nearby café.

As I sat there with my espresso, thinking of all the incredible art I'd miss out on seeing on account of Richie, he disrupted my train of thought.

"Them guys were jerks, man," he griped.

While sore at him for getting us in trouble, I held my tongue, knowing we'd be traveling together for two more weeks.

"Took all my film!" he continued to bitch, fiddling with his expensive camera.

Eleanor had sent me with a disposable Kodak. I was privileged in many ways, but my parents responded "no" when asked for nice things. Their Depression-era sensibility kept them from spoiling me.

In the morning, we boarded an ocean liner in the port of Civitavecchia. Accommodations were meager, intended to simulate the conditions Jews endured on their way to the concentration camps. When the vessel docked in Haifa that night, we were given a lecture on Zionism and ordered to run across a rocky terrain toward unmarked vans waiting to haul us to an unknown destination.

I was injured during that stampede and taken to an urgent care facility splattered with fresh blood droplets on the floors and bars on the windows. Released with a sprained wrist, I woke up coughing only hours later in an open tent on an Israeli army base and developed pneumonia. Our chaperones refused to close the tent flaps because they were trying to teach us what it was like to serve in the military.

As I groaned, Richie looked up from his comic book, reclining in the cot beside me.

"I don't know what you're complaining about, man. All this stuff was in the brochure," he joked, turning the page.

* * *

Fortunately, the last leg of our trip wasn't hellacious. We danced in Tel Aviv nightclubs, toured the Golan Heights, and floated in the Dead Sea. But the highlight was hiking Mount Masada in the Judean desert. When we reached that peak, I welcomed the sunrise in the ruins of a roofless temple.

Roman soldiers had discovered two Sicaraii rebels hiding there following a siege in 73 AD. The rest of the holdouts they'd been battling had committed suicide by throwing themselves off the mountain.

Legend had it that if you called out for a loved one at the cliffside, you might hear the names of the deceased echo back. I shouted my brother Albert's name, but all I heard was the chirp of a laughing dove. It perched a few feet from me on a jagged rock, hungering for its first worm of the morning.

Being of little faith, I dismissed it.

* * *

That Sunday, Richie and I set out to explore Jerusalem. He irritated me but was the only person on my tour willing to break the rules and try new things. We'd been cautioned to stay within a small radius of our hostel. Still, we defied the warning to comb the open-air market in the Arab quarter. Richie bought a drum he'd found in the first stall. He was itching to get back to the hostel and start banging on it when a young Arab stole it from his hands as we left the bazaar.

"Hey, give it back!" Richie whined in his southern drawl.

The man mocked him, passing the drum about with his friends like a volleyball.

"C'mon, give it back! I paid for that!"

Sensing trouble, a few shopkeepers receded from view.

"OK, Jew. I give. I give," the thief laughed, taunting Richie by dangling the instrument over his head.

"Hand it to me!" Richie cried, reaching for it.

"First, you dance, Jew," he scowled.

"Let's leave," I urged Richie.

"I want it, man. I paid for it," he squealed, parting his streaked blond hair with trembling fingers.

"You're not dancing for that stupid drum, Richie."

"If I do it for a couple minutes, maybe he'll give it back," he said on the verge of tears.

I didn't know him well, but I couldn't believe he'd let himself be so derided. Before I could say another word, he was dancing like a minstrel. The men cackled and chucked the drum at his feet. I could hardly bring myself to speak to him for the remainder of the trip.

* * *

I kept to myself the next day on a visit to the Wailing Wall, observing as men worshipped on one side and women on the other. It reminded me of Eleanor disrupting Ray's shul back in the fifties. A boy was getting bar mitzvah'd under the burning sun. I listened to his rabbi's blessings reverberate off the limestone blocks, folded prayers stuffed between them from end to end and as far as the arm could reach.

To the right, a ramp led into the Temple Mount, under Islamic control since the Six-Day War. Christians were allowed inside, but not Jews. Yet I'd come from halfway across the world and was determined to see it. So I wandered away from my group and headed in that direction. Seeing that no visitors walking up the incline wore head coverings, I removed my paisley bandana.

Two Arab soldiers at the entrance poked their rifles into my chest.

"*Qaf,*" they said sharply.

It means "stop" in Arabic.

"Can't I go in?" I asked plainly.

"Passport," they demanded.

I showed it to them. One soldier snagged it and waved over a senior officer. He evaluated my features like I was in a eugenics experiment. I guess I didn't look as Jewish as I could have. My hair was blond, and my eyes blue.

"Are you Jew?" the officer asked.

"Do I look like one?" I responded rhetorically.

He examined my nose, eyebrows, and hair more thoroughly but couldn't determine my ethnicity. Still, he was suspicious, so two guards escorted me in, one on each side. We walked just far enough for me to take in the view. Families picnicked on the grass at the foot of the temple's marble steps, and the newly minted Dome of the Rock glistened. It was so serene inside those walls that you could hear your innermost thoughts.

Ten seconds later, they threw me out.

But I was gratified I'd snuck past, and as I left, turned to the anti-semites and saluted them with a "*Shalom!*"

They snarled, knowing they'd been fooled.

* * *

My pneumonia relapsed on the last day of our trip while in the resort town of Eilat. I began hacking up phlegm and blood. I'd survive but was in bad shape. My brain was exhausted, wrestling with questions I'd never pondered. Why were so many people fighting and dying over the right to live here? What did the Middle East conflict mean to modern man? And was there really a God?

I limped along the beach, contemplating all this. And as the warm waves lapped at my ankles, I was overcome with both fear and wonder and fell to my knees, prostrating myself. Something about Israel was speaking to me, planting a seed of faith that would one day prove more fruitful than anything I'd ever harvest. It was the beginning of my most important journey, one I wouldn't fully appreciate until I had far more to lose in this life than I had to gain.

* * *

I sat by the wing on the flight home, grappling with those existential thoughts, when out of nowhere, a pigskin soared over my head. A tour group sharing our plane had become unruly. I'd seen them drinking in the airport, and within minutes of our departure could smell weed coming from their direction. Horny teenagers copulated in the seats in front of me, and another pair was getting busy in the lavatory. It was pandemonium. Even the stewardesses were getting their asses slapped as they pushed the drink cart.

Eventually, the captain exited the cockpit like a disgusted father and swore authorities would be waiting in LA. I lifted the window shade as our landing gear came down fifteen hours later. As promised, a dozen police cruisers, two fire engines, and an ambulance were racing along the runway. Revelers who hadn't yet passed out began to panic, knowing the party was over and judgment was coming.

But me? Well, I just sat there next to Richie, listening to *The Doors* on my Discman and watching him beat on that stupid drum.

* * *

I'd make up for whatever narcotics I missed out on during that smokey flight in the first year of college after my monster escaped. Calvin, my drug-dealing roommate, helped me unlock its cage. On weekends, we got stoned in Isla Vista, a beach town by the university. It had become a vortex for addicts, grifters, and grey-haired radicals who'd survived the sixties. The locals considered themselves veterans of that culture war, glamorizing the turbulent era as if they were modern-day Montagnards of the French Revolution.

They'd stopped Vietnam!
They burned their bras!
They impeached Nixon!

But the romanticized history they presented to new students had been grossly distorted by all the drugs they'd ingested. They omitted the unpleasant parts about overdoses, bank bombings, riots, kidnappings, broken homes, and other havoc. So, to wide-eyed freshmen like me, these fossilized hippies were nothing but wise heroes who valiantly fought The Man with daisies, LSD, and sitars—and had been victorious!

Regrettably, I was a card-carrying member of that protest club, fueled by an insidious, faux rage often stoked by my academic mentors. In the weekly column I penned for the school paper, *The Daily Nexus*, I called out the hypocrisy I perceived on campus. Yet while popular with the student body, my arguments were one-sided and mean. They mercilessly belittled institutions like the Greek system, which I lampooned as an assembly line of conformity.

But the monster inside me knew the truth.

The fanaticism I espoused in print was an outward expression of the discord stewing within me. Deep down, I envied the sense of belonging fraternities offered. Afraid of rushing and being rejected by them, I blockaded myself within a small sphere of influence at the paper. I never managed to step out of that bubble long enough to realize how out of touch I was.

In school, I listened bright-eyed through my professors' lectures on Hume, Locke, and Mill as if Aristotle himself was tutoring me. My teachers became my demigods, infallible and beyond reproach. As days passed, my worldview became a mélange of their arcane narratives, stitched together like a quilt—easy to wrap yourself in but too flimsy to keep you warm.

* * *

My friend, Thalia, was duped by that same liberal arts mirage. She lived in off-campus housing, and I'd regularly visit her with Calvin, who introduced us during orientation. She'd just moved into her apartment when we met and was sitting Indian style at the foot of her bed, a French pedicure peeking from beneath her toned calves.

"*Voilà,*" she said, kissing a joint she'd rolled and handing it to me.

This is the kind of girl I could marry and have kids with, I told myself.

She was such a lively, unstoppable young thing—redheaded, with hazel eyes and buck teeth like mine. Her hair was tied in pigtails, and she sucked on candy pacifiers, which drove me mad. Calvin and I fought for her attention as if she were Helen of Troy. And though she was a wild orchid, she'd seemed to come up smelling like roses, no matter what grew in her garden.

We were en route to pick up a bag from Thalia one day when half a dozen undercover cops raided her place. A crowd had gathered outside, gossiping about her fate, and we assumed it was curtains for the pixie. An hour later, the fuzz left empty-handed, *thanking her* as she stood barefoot in the doorframe, tying the belt of her silk kimono.

Thalia motioned to Calvin and me from down the hall and invited us in. She glossed over what had just happened and mentioned that she needed a date for a keg party that evening. Since Calvin's parents were visiting, I gladly accompanied her.

I'd finally got the girl to myself, I thought.

We talked all night and left the party holding hands. Staggering down the sidewalk, we passed a vacant lot where fragrant lavender peppered the breeze. An old sofa missing cushions had been junked near the bluffs overlooking the ocean. It was high tide, and waves shimmered in the moonlight as they crashed below.

"Raf, let's wait here for the sunrise," she whispered, pulling at my jacket.

We sat down, and Thalia rested her head on my shoulder. I cupped her dimpled chin and fell captive to her. Our lips were cold and moist as they kissed. Her eyes shut, and she walked her fingers down my chest. As her hand reached inside my stonewashed jeans, I kissed her neck. The rubber bands tying up her hair were gone, and I twisted her red mane around my wrist. She pulled back for a moment, and my heart skipped a beat. But then she bent toward me, unzipping my pants. I looked to the stars thinking my wish had been granted.

Suddenly, Thalia's head started oscillating like a drinking bird toy. And in one fell swoop, she hurled—all over me. I sat there like a plaster cast in Pompeii, the expression on my face frozen from the moment I met my demise. It was hard to see her the same way afterward. We'd remain friends, but romance was no longer in the cards.

I was young, fickle, and fell in love with everything. And every woman. They would come and go, but I was a perpetual victim of unrequited love. No coupling was ever light and ephemeral. My partners picked up on it, sending them heading for the hills before anything serious could develop. I crafted conclusions before climaxes, warping the natural arc every relationship traces before it either fails or succeeds.

My monster kept me chained to rejections of the past and from living in the now. It fed off my deep-seated fear of abandonment, still thinly veiled by the secret behind my adoption.

* * *

I wrote postcards to my best friend Kris every month, and he called me from LA whenever he had a break. He'd left the entertainment industry and taken a job at a magazine stand, often complaining how actors he'd once worked with would drop by to see what had become of him. It pained me to hear it. Kris deserved to go to college more than I ever did. But he never stood a chance, being shlepped from audition to audition. Besides, the tutors on his sets were sub-par, a parade of Hollywood wannabees who showed no interest in his development.

Sensing he was downtrodden, I invited him to live with me in Santa Barbara.

Within twenty-four hours of extending the offer, Kris was at my doorstep with his suitcase and an armful of Cal Tjader records. And it didn't take long for him to overstay the welcome. By week's end, he'd duct taped his Bruce Lee posters to my walls, eaten all my Ramen, and hung a rope hammock in my living room. I came home from class to find him dozing in it, a watch cap covering his eyes like he was between two palm trees.

I told him he could stay while finding a new place.

The following Saturday, he roused me at dawn. As was his custom, he'd traverse the block with a fresh cup of joe, sketching in a spiral notebook, or reading Robert Pirsig's *Zen and the Art of Motorcycle Maintenance.* He'd come across something interesting that morning and couldn't wait to show me.

"Rafie, come outside," he insisted, smacking me with his notebook and waking me from my slumber. "There's a hot chick on the carport."

I put on my jeans and followed him to the balcony, where he pointed out an alluring Taiwanese girl, dawdling there lithely.

"Hi!" she waved, using her other hand as a visor to block the rising sun. "I'm Mei. I live next door."

"What are you doing up there?" I asked.

"I came looking for my cat. And I kind of got stuck," she giggled, biting her bottom lip.

We promptly fetched a ladder and rescued her.

"Sorry to make you guys do all this," she apologized, carefully climbing down each rung. "Can I offer you some tea or something?"

We accepted her invitation without hesitation. When she opened the door to her apartment, it was cluttered and stunk of cat litter. Strewn about were piles of sundresses, half-burnt votive candles, and astronomy textbooks. A waterlogged guitar leaned against an upright piano in the corner. But the filth didn't seem to turn off Kris. It may have reminded him of his mother.

As she boiled some water, he confessed that he needed a new place to live. I admitted to being the cause of his homelessness. Neither statement made us look like boyfriend material. She handed us teacups and sat down.

"Why don't you come live here, Kris?" she asked unexpectedly, having known him less than an hour.

Kris spit out some of the hot tea she'd served.

"Here? With you?"

"Sure," she said, eyeing me. "I'm usually not even here because I'm studying or working at the library."

"Where in the library?" I asked.

"Wait. How much?" Kris interrupted.

"Whatever you can afford," she answered.

Kris readily accepted her sliding scale offer. Despite the decrepit conditions, he was enamored of the girl. We both were. She was like a pretty flower in a dung heap. Sometime later, we learned she was actually an heiress, the only daughter of a millionaire from Taipei. But living like a slob didn't seem to bother the rich girl. And the one thing she loved more than making a mess was that cat. After two days, she still hadn't found the poor thing.

While Kris moved his stuff in, Mei and I papered the neighborhood with flyers. After the third day of fruitless searching, she started crying for the little calico—all she had in the States. When we returned to her place, she ran to her bedroom, and I followed. As I comforted her, we heard the tiniest *meow.* I peeked behind the dresser she'd shoved in her closet, and beneath a pile of dirty clothes was that kitty.

Mei was overjoyed. And kissed me!

Soon after, I lost my innocence to that catwoman in the hammock Kris had hung. It marked a new chapter in my life but was a betrayal for Kris. He was wroth when he learned of us, swearing he'd never forgive me. While he never had a chance with Mei, he told himself I'd swooped in and seized her like a hawk.

One day when he left his notebook out, I flipped through a few journal entries, reading his operatic descriptions of how my arms around her shoulders were "like talons" and her lips "should have been his." He was justifiably pissed that he had to live with her in that putrid apartment while we cavorted next door.

* * *

The strain took its toll on my relationship with Mei, torpedoing it. Right before we split, though, she helped me get a job in the special collections department of the university library. I needed the work. Eleanor and Ray had covered my rent in school, but I'd taken out loans to pay for tuition and was expected to make up the balance of the monthly nut. The gig was a dream come true for an aspiring writer, located on a quiet floor mainly accessed by scholars who kept to themselves. If literature were gold, a job in special collections was like having the keys to Fort Knox.

In the back of the archives, a refrigerated, steel vault preserved priceless artifacts, including a fifteenth-century Gutenberg Bible, the first edition of *Leaves of Grass*, and an autographed copy of William Blake's *The Marriage of Heaven and Hell*. My favorite band, The Doors, was named after a line in that 1794 masterpiece that read, "If the doors of perception were cleansed, everything would appear to man as it is, infinite."

That was how the library felt—infinite.

The east wing housed an American Religions collection, a trove of contemporary books and journals representing every Christian denomination in North America. I wasn't much interested. Yet the

Bible had always commanded my respect. That timeless opening—*In the beginning, God created the heavens and the earth, and the earth was unformed and void, and darkness was upon the face of the waters, and God said, let there be light*—it mystified and enraptured me.

We knew so little of the cosmos when those scrolls were written. Yet, the passage sounded like a lucid description of the big bang. Even the sequence of events in the creation story seemed *evolutionary*. How could mortals have postulated such an astonishing theory so many millennia ago? And why did the universe continue to bury its secrets so deep, unbeknownst to us, revealing them only at a time and place of its choosing? Was there not a kernel of truth to it?

I would have spent more time asking questions like that had I not been drawn to the Darwin Collection in the library's west wing. Its diverse texts spanned the Enlightenment through the publication of *The Origin of Species*. I became mesmerized, going so far as to sneak out "reading room only" materials. As I leafed through one publication, *The Evolution of the Idea of God*, the words of its author Grant Allen displaced me:

> I propose in this work to trace out in rough outline the evolution of the idea of God from its earliest and crudest beginnings in the savage mind of primitive man to that highly evolved and abstract form which it finally assumes in contemporary philosophical and theological thinking.

God—an idea? A mere philosophy born from the brain of primitive man? I'd never thought of it so scientifically or heard it stated so adamantly. To Allen, the notion of a deity was an abstraction, a work of complete fiction with no basis in empirical fact. And yet, the author felt he needed to dedicate numerous books and much of his career to exploring that *idea*.

I was reminded of my trip to Israel.

There too, as I stood atop Mount Masada, I'd struggled to reconcile an illustrious biblical narrative with the record in the rocks. Allen's argument was compelling, but I couldn't lightly dismiss how the faithful people in my life, from my parents to Mr. Hale, had steered me in the right direction. They'd imbued it with more meaning and depth than Allen could ever offer. And most of their wisdom came from the Bible, not science.

Still, I was lost. And too shortsighted to see that, like secularists, I'd misconstrued faith as blind trust in ancient men's words rather than a recognition of the sublime force which divinely inspired their myths. We're destined to feel deceived if we accept the premise that our origin stories have been *designed* to deceive us. If, on the other hand, we acknowledge myth as wisdom's aesthetic, we're equipped to embrace and receive it like the gift that it is.

But as a young man, I was cocksure, unable to spool the common thread tying together all faiths—a desire for peace, happiness, and purpose. I couldn't see the Garden of Eden through all the trees cut down to make those damned library books! By semester's end, I'd read whole shelves of the Darwin Collection and grown cynical of anything remotely associated with religion. Yet the fountain that sprang from the well of natural selection couldn't quench my thirst. I was desperate to taste a different elixir.

* * *

That's the moment I met Delilah—an aspiring poet with a wistful smile and heart-shaped face that she hid behind her curly black bangs. She practically lived at our local coffee shop, smoking bidis around the clock while reading Sylvia Plath. And no matter how hot it got, she'd wear a red Moto jacket each day, her nose in that same depressing book.

She never looked up.

At the time, I lived with a roadie for the Allman Brothers Band named Rob. We'd met at a burrito stand, and after hearing how he was down on his luck, I heedlessly offered to let him crash at my place. Much like Kris, he ate my groceries and drank my beer. He was certifiably feral, reeking like a patchouli factory. And while he never paid rent, his free spirit was infectious.

I was also a little afraid to ask him to leave.

Despite his head-to-toe motorcycle gang tattoos and a lengthy rap sheet, Rob was a life-sized teddy bear. You could talk to the guy about anything. After venting about how lost I felt one day after class, he said all I was missing was companionship. In his forty-some years of experience, *primarily with groupies*, not having enough love in your life kept you from being happy. He suggested I buy him a beer so he could elaborate.

As we walked toward the brewery debating the matter, I spotted Delilah. She was resplendent, wearing a white camisole, her hair tied back, and sitting at a different table for once, without her book.

"That's her, isn't it?" he asked loudly, pointing tactlessly.

"No," I lied, my stomach filling up with butterflies.

"Yup. That's her, bro," he confirmed, swinging his big arm around my shoulders and plowing us toward Delilah.

She looked amused as he started waving, and I knew it was too late to back out.

"Hey there," my matchmaker said confidently. "Mind if we sit down, babe?"

"I'm waiting for somebody, but he's not coming for a—"

"The wait is over, babe. The dude's right here," Rob smiled, forcing me to sit next to her and presenting me like a game-show prize.

She laughed as Rob sang my praises, charming the pants off her. He was adamant that we were destined to be a couple. A day later, his prophecy was fulfilled, and we were under the covers. I lost all track of time. I started missing classes, and my grades dropped. But I didn't care. Delilah was everything to me. A month after Rob went back on the road, I asked her to move in.

We spent almost every evening from that point tied up like a pretzel on my lumpy futon, reading William Burroughs, Diane di Prima, Lawrence Ferlinghetti, and trying to memorize Allen Ginsberg's *Howl*. We lived vicariously through those beatniks, though our late nights were less memorable. Often they were little more than a six-pack, some lovin', and a trip to Joe's Café for the French dip. And things changed after she started probing me about my career plans, of which I had none.

All I was sure of was that I wanted to become a writer.

* * *

I'd confided to Delilah that Eleanor disapproved of my English major, insisting I pursue something more practical.

"Rafie, life is too short not to follow your dreams!" she said, firing up another bowl on the balcony, the freeway whirring two blocks away. "Don't let *that woman* stop you."

She told me what I wanted to hear. That Monday, I left the apartment inspired and called Delilah from the payphone outside the dean's office, boasting that I'd quit school to write the great American novel.

"That's a big move, Raf," she said, her voice trailing.

"I know. Well, go big or go home, right?" I replied, lighting a cigarette.

"Uh-huh," Delilah muttered timidly.

Anxiously, I hurried back home, excited to start bouncing story ideas off her. But when I threw open the door, she was gone. She'd taken her toothbrush and all her weed and left me a Post-it note on the fridge, saying I'd misunderstood what she meant by following my dreams.

What she meant was to follow them *after* finishing college—*after*. My impulsivity had scared her off.

I was heartbroken.

My gut sank, and my head began to swirl. I ran to the bathroom, thinking I would vomit, feeling like I'd lost everything. As I splashed cold water on my cheeks, I stared hard at myself in the vanity. It had been forever since I took a good look at my face. Since suffering from cystic acne, I'd avoided all mirrors and even my reflection while passing windows on the street. And because I resembled a monster throughout my adolescence, it kept me from looking deeper, past my complexion, and into my soul.

Now that my acne was gone, I could see the beast beneath the surface. I'd seen it in others but could no longer ignore the one inside me. I'd aided and abetted it for years, feeding it dope and delusions—appeasing it. I knew the time had finally come to deal with it, but I didn't know how.

Distraught and confused, I redirected my energy toward Delilah, pledging to win her back. A few hours later, channeling Jack Kerouac, I'd broken my lease, gotten on the road, and followed the signs to San Francisco.

Quests

Dropping out of school was reckless and yet liberating. As I hightailed it up the idyllic and winding Pacific Coast Highway, I replayed those garrulous nights with Delilah, scrutinizing the Beats. I was convinced I'd found my artistic direction in one of them—Lawrence Ferlinghetti. Unlike the roundtable of insolent writers he'd been jailed for publishing, the tall Italian was an old soul, forbearing and patently masculine. A half-century later, with his closest contemporaries dead and gone, he still held court at his famed City Lights bookstore.

I parked in North Beach at midday and walked into the shop. It was well-trafficked yet quiet. A steep, narrow stairwell to the poetry section creaked with each step. Climbing up, you could smell the pulp resting on the redwood bookshelves. I was awestruck by the history of the place and its spooky vibration. Authors' spirits lining the shelves seemed to be calling out from their literary graves, "Read this, read this, you bastard child!"

I heard a toilet flush down a hallway, and a door opened. An elderly man exited, walking placidly in my direction. He saw me browsing a stream-of-consciousness novel entitled *Her*. Deliberately taking it from my hands, he replaced it with *A Coney Island of the Mind*, a short book of poems.

"Start with that one," he suggested, patting my shoulder.

"Any good?" I asked, staring at the cover.

"It's okay," he replied, departing downstairs.

I flipped through the pages. It was published in 1958, the year Albert was born.

"I shall buy it," I thought. "The old man must know what he's talking about."

At the cash register, the clerk, a gangly twenty-something in a black suit, set down his copy of *Women in Love* and began to ring me up. Right behind him, the man I'd seen upstairs grabbed his jacket from the coat rack, brushing by me accidentally as he left. As I paid for the book, it occurred to me that I might ask to see Ferlinghetti, the shop owner.

"I know this sounds strange," I told the clerk, "but I've come a long way. Do you think I can speak to Lawrence Ferlinghetti?"

"Just left," he said, handing me my change.

"No kidding?"

"Yeah. No kidding," he replied, annoyed.

"When?" I asked as if I had some right to know.

"While you were jabbering," he added, not missing a beat.

I turned around, and through the shop's stenciled glass, I saw the bearded proprietor *who'd just sold me his own book* climbing Columbus Avenue. He wore a fisherman's cap, casually walking his pooch, Whitman. The man must have been about eighty but moved with a spring in his step. I ran outside and caught up to him as he entered the crosswalk.

"Mr. Ferlinghetti!" I shouted without having planned what to say next.

"Hello," he answered unassumingly.

I was likely not the first random to stalk the laureate on his afternoon dog walk.

"I've come all the way here, Mr. Ferlinghetti. From Santa Barbara," I said, out of breath.

"Oh my. What is that, about a five-hour drive?" the poet responded wryly.

"For a woman," I clarified. "She inspired me—to become a writer like you. She's planning to join me one of these days. I think."

"You think?"

"Yes, I'm waiting for her."

"Waiting?"

"Yeah. What do you think I should do?" I asked.

"How the hell should I know?" he responded, pulling his dog off the curb.

"I thought maybe—"

"Look, kid. It all depends on what you're waiting for."

His index finger tapped the cover of the book I'd purchased.

"There's a poem in there. All about waiting," Ferlinghetti said before crossing the street.

I followed his silhouette until it disappeared into a crowd of pedestrians and opened the book to the poem he mentioned. The poet's words and his vibrant city enthralled me. I decided to stay awhile but had no tangible assets except the car I drove up. So, I sold it in the online classifieds. With the money, I put two months' rent down on a windowless studio on Sixth and Market. It was Skid Row. I slept on a mattress on the unfinished floor, ferociously working on my novel day and night—an incoherent rambling that would make the Unabomber blush.

I was a fool by every measure, but I was my own fool. And in charge of my own destiny. I wasn't yet moving in the right direction, but at least I was moving beyond my sense of entitlement. And that was *progress.*

* * *

Though I was flat broke, the economy was on an upswing thanks to the dot-com boom. Venture capitalists were dumping millions into hair-brained start-ups to nowhere, but some of today's big tech companies were also being born. Many were headquartered in San Francisco. And I, against my mother's advice, had pursued an English major.

I remained unemployed.

Typing sixty-five words a minute was my one marketable skill. Yet, I didn't even have enough work experience to get my foot in the door as an office assistant. My job at the library didn't cut it either. Entry-level office work was intended for new graduates, and everything else required qualifications I didn't possess. I was running low on cash, and the city's lights were dimming fast, like a row of streetlamps shutting off at dawn.

I'd made only one friend in San Francisco—a cheery Irish bloke with a round, red balloon face who lived across the hall. He worked the door at the Saint Francis Drake hotel, dressed in a Beefeater, and encouraged me to apply for the morning shift.

"No experience needed to open a door, Rafie," he'd say, adding that hours were flexible and the benefits generous.

Once in a while, he'd pull out a crisp hundred-dollar bill a guest had tipped him, waving it in my face like he'd won the lotto.

"A few more of these, and I'll be able to create *Bildungsroman*," he'd say, proudly folding up the greenback.

Bildungsroman. It was the name of the role-playing game he'd been designing, from which he hoped to one day grow rich. Had I bothered to finish college, I might have known what that term meant, but at the time, I just assumed it was his gaming avatar. Often he'd invite me to his cosplay events, although I never accepted. He'd wear full regalia, including a cape, always bidding me adieu in character as he departed for the charade.

I was indebted to the guy for getting me the interview, so I agreed to meet him at the hotel and give it a shot. But as I approached the Powell Street entrance the next morning on the cable car, I saw him in that obnoxious Beefeater costume. He stood erect like a Buckingham Palace guard. I sheepishly moved to the opposite side of the trolley, where he couldn't see me. While desperately needing a job, I'd stopped wearing costumes in high school.

With little left in my pockets, I walked down Market Street to my favorite bakery, stretching my dollar drip coffee into the afternoon. I picked up the *Guardian*, the free weekly paper, noticing a quarter-page ad for the Jackson Personnel Agency located a block away. They took walk-ins. So, without a resume and nothing to lose, I strode into Arthur Jackson's office, just as Mom had into Donald Sterling's back in the seventies.

"Have a seat," Mr. Jackson said, directing me to a tufted leather chair without looking up.

I sat there for twenty minutes before he uttered another word.

He was in his early fifties but wizened like he'd been doing business since the 1906 earthquake. In a corner was the wheelchair he'd been relegated to after an illness had left him disabled. But it didn't seem to have slowed the man down. Hung on the walls behind him were tokens of his past success—dozens of photographs with athletes and celebrities and embossed accolades he'd received from the city.

"That's Willie Brown. Willie Brown. Mayor," he noted, scribbling something on his stationery and handing it to a temp. "Appointed me Health Commissioner. Health Commissioner," he reiterated.

Mr. Jackson hadn't yet introduced himself, and I wasn't sure how to respond.

"Okay. What's your name, young man?" he asked.

"Rafael," I replied affirmatively.

"Rafee-el? C'mon, what's your real name, son?"

"That's my name, sir."

"Was your momma trying to punish you?" he joked, putting down his pen.

"It was going to be Bucky," I smiled.

I could tell I'd won him over by the way he laughed at the comment.

"Can you type?"

"Sixty-five words a minute," I boasted.

"Good. You want a job?"

"Yes. Thank you!" I replied, leaning forward.

He wrote down an address and handed it to me.

"Montgomery Street. Data Entry. Dress professionally. No tie. No tie."

I started bright and early the next day, keying data into a spreadsheet. Everything seemed normal until I was about to take my break. But as I stepped outside my cubicle, the sexy, coquettish supervisor I reported to grabbed my shoulder and forced me back into my chair.

"You can take a break when it's over," she said under her breath, adjusting her brassiere.

"When—what is over?" I asked, enjoying the false imprisonment.

She leaned in closer and whispered in my ear, "We're getting a special visit from the CEO of limousine dot-com."

"Who?" I asked, having never heard of the company.

She shushed me as silence fell over the repurposed warehouse, where we'd assembled like a doomsday cult about to drink the punch. The door swung open, and a man-child swaggered in, wearing an oversized white suit and accompanied by a small entourage. His name was announced as if he were the Commander in Chief, and employees broke into spirited applause. I turned to my supervisor, who was clapping like a zealot from a Nazi propaganda film.

"I'll be right back," I told her, taking my coat and skedaddling.

* * *

I passed the Rizzoli bookstore on Post Street on my way home. Its display windows were decorated with Christmas wreaths, gold-trimmed red ribbons, and coffee-table books on subjects too refined for my palette. Peering through the glass doors, I pictured the day I might be able to afford something inside when I'd finally made it.

An elegant woman, well into her sixties, slowly wrapped books at a counter in the back. She turned and smiled, calling me in with her wrinkled hand. I accepted the invitation and walked toward where she sat on a stool, almost motionless, like the Oracle of Delphi. Standing there like a supplicant, I waited for her to proclaim something.

"Hi there," she said, tying a bow.

"Hi," I replied, elated she was speaking to me.

Until then, life in the city had been inauspicious. I was penniless, and my neighborhood was so dicey that you couldn't even walk it after dusk. The stores were all boarded up each night except for the peep shows, pawnshops, and liquor marts. I hoped to move somewhere safer once I had a steady job. But I had little to offer, even in terms of conversation. Somehow this Black woman standing in front of me knew that. It was like she'd been chosen to foster me or seen so many tenderfoots staring through those windows that she'd developed a reflex.

"We're hiring," she said, handing me an application.

"You are?"

"Do you have any experience working in bookstores?"

"I worked at a library. Does that count?" I asked humbly.

"Go ahead, mark it down right there," the woman replied. "I'll be just a minute."

She got up gracefully. I watched as she put in a good word with the manager, a middle-aged, overworked man with a high turnover. He called me into his office and offered me the position later that week.

For the next six months, I'd sit with that demure woman, Nella, day after day, usually in silence, wrapping books for the San Francisco bourgeoisie. Every once in a while, I'd listen to her reminisce. She'd been a singer and dancer, a promising disciple of the Josephine Baker school. But her wings were clipped by a panderer before she got a chance to fly.

Nella said she'd met him in the Fillmore district while running in the same circles as Etta James. On some days, I imagine she even looked like Etta, with sleepy eyes that guarded the cauldron of secrets she kept living on those mean streets. Her abuser was shot dead in the Tenderloin in nineteen eighty-something, but his killer was never found. His death freed Nella, though she'd lost the best years of her life. Now she was just a delicate antique—about the most beautiful thing you could find in that ornate bookstore.

I'd lost contact with the rest of my family, so Nella was like a mother to me. Her kindness on the dayshift is what helped me pass the lonely nights. At home, I would eat fast food and diligently tackle my masterpiece until I fell asleep. When I finished the final draft, I sent it to every publisher accepting new material. Rejection letters came back expeditiously. I was chastened and complained to Nella at work about how crappy it made me feel.

"That's okay, sweet pea. You never been published, and it probably wasn't that good of a book anyway," Nella teased, grabbing her handbag as she prepared to leave for the day.

She then turned to me and said, "Rafee-el."

"Yes, Nella," I responded.

"Don't worry too much about that book of yours. You're young. You can try again."

"Okay," I said, smiling as she hobbled away.

She paused by the glass doors through which I'd first observed her, bracing her ribcage as she left for the evening. In the morning, I was called in to cover her shift. She'd passed in the night, peacefully in her sleep, and back to the heavens from which she came.

* * *

Bookstore wages couldn't cover my rent, so I invited Kris to San Francisco to share the studio. Our fight over Mei was well behind us. And because he had residual income from his child actor days, we were able to get by month-to-month. I even agreed to let him put up his Bruce Lee posters but refused to let him drill holes for another hammock—there wasn't room.

We didn't see much of each other once I started working double shifts at the bookstore. Shortly after Nella died, the manager reassigned me to the self-help section. It's where I first met Jennie, a curvy Pacific Islander with caramel skin and a short black bob. She had a movie-star smile, high cheekbones, and a nasty habit of chewing the jumbo straws from the smoothie shop next door. Her days were spent reading alone on the Berber carpet in my section, and she didn't leave until closing.

One night Jennie waited outside for over an hour until I settled the register, sneaking up on me as I locked up.

"Aren't you going to say hi?" she asked, smoking a clove.

My brand was Marlboro. She somehow knew that and had bought me a pack.

"Pay me back later," she said seductively, sliding the cigarettes into my shirt pocket.

It had been a scorcher, and we hiked up Stockton Street to a dive bar, getting acquainted over mint juleps. I hadn't the faintest clue that she was in the middle of a manic episode or that I was becoming her obsession. And since I hadn't dated anybody since Delilah, I savored the attentiveness as we wobbled home.

All of a sudden, she began yanking at random car door handles on the street until she found an unlocked one—on a 1960s Mustang fastback.

"Whoa, Jennie. It's somebody's ride," I cautioned.

She ignored my admonishment, bending the passenger seat forward and pushing me into the back seat. The door shut behind us, and she mounted me like a bucking horse, digging her heels into my thighs like stirrups. The hot leather was still warm from the sun earlier that day. Sweat on my neck stuck to it as she guided my hand, biting me carnally.

I hadn't done it in a car, let alone one that didn't belong to me. But it was more private than the tiny box I shared with Kris. So I returned the affection, spellbound by her euphoric expressions and the moonlight shining through the rear window.

"Keep going," she panted as the windows fogged up.

"We just met. Slow down."

"No, fuck me," she demanded.

I ripped open her blouse, unbuckled her jeans, and we made love.

Afterward, as we sat there, curled up like a couple of cherubs, a cop pulled up. He stepped out of the patrol car and poked in his flashlight.

"What's going on here? You alright, young lady?"

"It's okay, officer. I'm fine," Jennie reassured him. "This is my car."

He took her at her word, returned to his vehicle, and drove off. We deserted the Mustang, caught a cab to my place, and conked out.

I woke to the smell of frying bacon. Jennie was cooking breakfast with Kris and sharing bawdy details of our romp.

"What's up, Rafie?" Kris said as he came and sat at the foot of my mattress.

"Yo," I replied, rubbing the sleep from my eyes.

"Who is this amazing woman?"

"Uh—not sure yet."

Jennie left too many hours later. I called her that night and suggested again that we cool it. But she showed up at the bookstore the very next morning. Her fixation grew more and more problematic with each passing day. She would arrive when the doors opened and wouldn't leave until they closed. My manager insisted I do something, so I took Jennie outside and tried to let her down.

She became hysterical, and ignoring her made it even worse.

Later that evening, she followed me home, confronting me outside my tenement. Without any provocation, she flailed her arms, bashing me repeatedly. I covered my face as she hit me, explaining that I'd almost lost my job due to her antics, but she didn't care. She wrapped her arms around a parking meter and fell to her knees. I knew the girl needed help, but I could barely help myself. Wiping her tears, she kissed me and said one "last" goodbye.

Rattled, I unlocked my studio door and crawled into Kris' bed since he'd passed out drunk in mine. Closing my eyes, I pictured my future working at the bookstore until my dying day, like Nella. I'd be consigned to wrapping gift books for the rich and passing out job applications to younger facsimiles of myself.

So be it, I thought. *I have made this bed, and now I shall lie in it.*

As I was dozing, I heard footsteps outside. The door handle turned slightly, but I assumed it was a neighbor who'd mistaken where they lived. I dismissed it and had just fallen back asleep when someone managed to break in. Suddenly, I felt a shoe on my groin, and the intruder plopped onto my chest like a gargoyle fallen from a skyscraper. I yelped, thinking I was being attacked.

It was only Jennie. *Kris had cut her a key.*

"Hi," she whispered.

"Jennie? What the hell!"

Kris woke up and flipped on a light.

"Hey, Kris," she said as if nothing had happened.

"Can't take this anymore!" I yelled, heaving Jennie off me.

I collected my things hastily—a couple of duffle bags with clothes and my laptop. Jennie begged me not to leave as Kris watched keenly.

"Where are you going?" he inquired as I lit a smoke.

"Time to go home," I answered, giving him a wad of cash I'd been saving.

"Should I look for a new roommate?" he asked, uncertain how he'd afford the apartment.

"Whatever you think, man," I replied, hugging my old friend before stepping into the hallway and leaving Jennie inside alone with him.

"She's nuts, you know," he shouted from the door as I called the elevator.

He was right, and after I left San Francisco, Kris took her in. Weeks later, he sent me a heartfelt letter after they'd fallen in love.

> Raf, once you were gone, I was talking alone with Jennie. She understands my paranoia about my scoliosis. The girls I've known, I've tried to see if they would understand, but their answer would be, "does it hurt" or "can't you get that fixed?" Pretty much, they didn't call me. I had to get them past my body and into my mind. Does it take a crazy woman to accept me? Maybe. The love I believe my guy friends have for me and what I am, I have now found in this girl. You took mine (Mei). I took yours. I hope you can be happy for us. —Kris

My life was in disarray, but I was happy for Kris, who'd always gotten the short end of the stick. He'd found somebody to love him the way he deserved. Still, I was concerned because both he and Jennie had addictive personalities. Would they continue to love and support each other, or end up like so many other friends who lost their lives to the monster?

We lost touch, and I never really saw them again.

***

That night, I rested my forehead on the chilly Greyhound window, preparing for the browbeating I expected from my parents. Given all

I'd done, I wasn't sure they'd even accept me back—quitting school and moving to San Francisco to become a poet. I'd realized I was no Lawrence Ferlinghetti, missed them terribly, and was contrite.

When I arrived at Eleanor's gates at two a.m., a light went on in her bedroom, and she groggily came downstairs to let me in. She spared me a tongue lashing, accompanying me to my bedroom with her usual suggestion that we talk about it later.

Ray hovered over me as I took off my shoes and jacket.

"How was your little adventure, Rafie?"

"I finished my book, Dad," I replied, hoping he'd ask a follow-up.

"Go to bed," he huffed, shaking his bald head and closing the door behind him.

I knew my folks were displeased, but looking around, I felt safe for the first time in months. I sat down at my white lacquer desk by the window. On it, Mom had arranged childhood mementos and photographs she'd retrieved from deep inside the drawers, displaying them like an exhibit of the life I led before my corruption.

My parents loved me immensely but never registered how lost I was. They'd concealed my adoption so long ago that they couldn't understand what I needed—to get home. And not to their four walls but to a place where I could be comfortable in my own skin.

* * *

In the morning, I ran errands in the Cadillac with Dad just like we used to when Tony was around. He'd upgraded to a new model, and I asked if he missed the old wheels. But Dad hadn't yet forgiven my transgression. He made a snide remark about how I needed to get my act together, and the rest of the ride kept quiet.

His radio was tuned to a news station reporting a heinous crime from the previous day. An unhinged motorist had picked a fight with a driver who'd rear-ended him, stolen a poodle off her lap, and launched it into oncoming traffic.

"What a schmuck," Dad said as we stopped at the light.

"You don't know the whole story," I replied insensitively.

My father's eyes lit up. The second the signal turned green, he accelerated, pulling to the curb a mile from our house. I thought he would beat me like that guy who'd tried to steal his parking ticket.

"What is the matter with you, son?"

"What? Maybe the guy had a good reason," I continued arguing.

"There's *never* a good reason to throw a poodle into traffic!" he yelled. "Get out of this car before I knock your teeth out."

"Fine!" I replied, slamming the door.

I watched as he drove off. When it came to conflict resolution, Ray hadn't changed much, and neither had I. Over the previous two weeks, he'd become irate. And not just with me. He was perturbed by a brooding man in black who'd been circling the block. The stranger would come and go about the same time each day, dragging his feet, mumbling and flicking the long bangs that covered his purple bifocals.

As Dad pulled into our driveway that afternoon, he almost ran over the guy, who raised his hand, garbling something unintelligible. Dad shook his head and called the police. Two cops rang our doorbell as I arrived home from my unscheduled walk.

"Mr. Moscatel?" the lead officer asked.

"Gimme a minute," Ray replied before pointing at me. "You. Go to your room."

I snuck around and eavesdropped from the top of the stairs.

"Mr. Moscatel, we checked on that guy you called about."

"Okay, so?" Dad said, staring at the men.

"Sir, there's been a misunderstanding," the officer continued, looking at his partner with a dumb grin. "He's your new neighbor—Ozzy!"

"Am I supposed to know *who that is?*" Dad asked.

"Ozzy Osbourne," the officer attempted to clarify. "He's a rock star, sir. He's like really famous. Lives in Mr. Marciano's old place."

But Ray didn't register the name. Unless it was an old movie star or an athlete, he didn't pay much attention to pop culture.

"Never heard of him," Dad shrugged as he shut the door.

Twenty-four hours later, a delightful British woman was at our doorstep with her two children. Our maid answered and let them in.

"Señora. Some lady here to see you," she called over the intercom to Mom, smiling at the well-mannered family.

They waited patiently for Eleanor as she descended the stairs.

"Hello there," Mom said cordially.

"Hello. We're your new neighbors. I'm Sharon," the ginger-haired lady replied in cockney.

In all the years Eleanor lived in Beverly Hills, she couldn't remember one time anyone had stopped by to introduce themselves. She invited the family into the living room and called for Dad and me. We came downstairs to greet them, sitting on the old tweed couches Mom had just reupholstered in beige leather.

"Ray, this is Sharon. You called the police on her husband yesterday, remember?"

"The wanderer?" Dad asked, cleaning his gums with a toothpick.

"Yes, but it's perfectly alright. I'm sorry if Ozzy frightened you. He likes to walk."

Sharon's kids stared at the numerous portraits of my brother Albert on the shelves. They could have been cast as Wednesday and Pugsley Addams.

Mom smiled at the boy, sporting a brown perm and glasses.

"What's your name?" she asked, like a grandma about to give him candy.

"M'name's Jack," he retorted with the tenor of a full-grown man.

"What school do you go to, Jack?"

"I don't go to school," the boy stated matter-of-factly.

"Neither do I," concurred his sister, Kelly.

"They do homeschooling," Sharon explained. And then, looking at me, asked Eleanor, "Is this your grandchild?"

"No, this is my son, Rafie," Mom declared.

"Oh, forgive me," apologized Sharon.

The comment was jarring. It wasn't the first time someone had pointed out our age difference. Still, it got me thinking again about how Mom would have been forty-six when she had me, an unlikely scenario in the 1970s.

In the first days after I was born, Eleanor went so far as to stage photos of herself pregnant, with a balloon under her dress in place of a bulging belly. That masquerade worked for years. But after Sharon made the observation, I started asking more questions. So Mom decided it was best to tweak her original contrivance that she birthed me, concocting a new "test-tube baby" story in its stead.

She now *admitted* that I was created *in vitro.*

Using her acting talents and cunning, I naively accepted the ploy.

* * *

Before I knew it, though, my parents and I were arguing incessantly again, and I'd begun to think it was a mistake to have come home. I took the first job I could find as a barista at Peet's Coffee & Tea and was consistently inept. Customers never got their orders right.

But when I was hired, the manager told us we had "flexibility" since the store was new. I broadly interpreted that to mean we could give the coffee away for free—along with beans, pastries, and French presses.

Maybe that's why nobody complained about the drinks.

Nobody except Bruce Paltrow—my favorite customer. The first time

I took his order, he joked that he wasn't actress Gwyneth Paltrow's father, with whom he shared the name but merely a dry cleaner with a caffeine habit. So I thought passing him off as the movie star's father might be fun. For weeks, I told every aspiring screenwriter who walked into the café about our "special customer."

"Hey, you know who that guy is over there?" I'd quiz them.

"No, who?" they'd ask.

"That's Mr. Paltrow. *The* Bruce Paltrow," I'd say, handing them their cappuccinos.

"Who?" they'd wonder.

"Gwyneth's dad," I'd whisper. "Be nice when you approach him. He is very powerful in this town."

"Okay, okay," they'd promise, thinking they had an inside tip.

Soon, more screenwriters started pouring in, hoping to bump into the bigwig. After a few weeks, the attention became too much, and Bruce walked up to me at the espresso machine.

"Rafael. Can we talk?" he asked, scratching his chin.

"Sure, Bruce," I replied, cleaning my steam wand. "What's up?"

"Got all these weirdos, you know, gawking at me while I'm drinking my coffee. And I've been asking myself, for weeks, like, what's going on?

"No shit?" I said with a telling grin.

"Are you sayin' I'm Gwyneth Paltrow's father?"

We laughed, and just as I agreed to end the stunt, my manager interrupted us.

"Excuse me, *Mr. Paltrow*," he said to Bruce before asking that I join him in his office.

I leaned against the wall in my apron as he logged into his computer.

"Listen, Rafael. I want everyone to be themselves around here, but keep business separate from pleasure, okay? Especially with famous guys like Bruce Paltrow," he stressed, oblivious to the hoax.

"My bad," I said. "Is that it?"

"No. Rafael, I brought you back here because we need to discuss something important."

I'd passed the probationary period, and he lauded my performance. But when I petitioned for a raise, he explained the job was a minimum wage for at least another six months. I argued that business would drop off sharply without me, and he injudiciously committed to going up the chain.

A week later, he called me back in.

"Good news, Rafael. I had to fight for it, but I got you that raise."

I was excited until he handed me a note with the corporate logo that read, *Approved: Additional 25 cents per hour.*

"This a joke, man?" I asked, rereading it.

"Is a joke five hundred and twenty dollars extra per year, Rafael? *Before taxes?"*

I took off my apron, handed it to him, and left.

On my way out, I passed Bruce, sitting under a peach umbrella on the patio. Hoping to help, he proposed an alternate route to success, an internship with a real Hollywood producer he knew. He thought it might turn into a full-time position if I proved myself. I took him up on the offer and interviewed at the Culver City offices of Alex Kitman Ho, a financier for Oliver Stone. At first, I was exhilarated because he'd bankrolled one of my favorite movies, *The Doors*. But all I did for the next month was answer his phones in exchange for the *privilege* of being in his presence.

I would have had better luck pressing shirts for the real Bruce Paltrow.

* * *

One bright spot was that I'd landed a writing agent, Robin Kaver of The Robert Freedman Agency in New York. She agreed to shop one of my scripts, a story about a third-grader who inherits a major film studio. I'd conjured up the "high concept" hook after being informed by writers at the coffee shop that I couldn't get representation trying to pen the sequel to *Hamlet.*

Being represented made me feel like I'd achieved some modicum of success, and I was jubilant. My parents, however, were fuming because I still couldn't hold a steady job. I'd relapsed into my writing addiction, experimenting with something nobody in LA had ever tried—screenplays! After fighting over what I would do with my future with the same intensity from when I was a teenager, they'd had enough.

It was the last straw, and they disinherited me.

It should have come as no surprise. Eleanor and Ray always had purposefully denied me certain fruits of their labor, in stark contrast to how Scotty Sterling's parents spoiled him. In my youth, I resented their frugality and assumed they owed me a share of their wealth. It made me a prodigal son. And like the parable, I wouldn't learn the lesson they were trying to impart until I'd had a chance to spread my wings and find my own nest.

* * *

I purchased a bus ticket back to San Francisco.

My former college roommate Calvin picked me up at the Mission Street terminal in his white jeep. He was wearing a rasta cap, puffing on a blunt, and blasting Kool Keith's *I Don't Believe You*. The rap song typified Calvin's misanthropic outlook. Like me, he'd been unprepared for college and dropped out. After leaving Santa Barbara, he took his drug dealing up north and built an extensive clientele. I wasn't privy to his business when I moved in, though I sensed something wasn't kosher.

It became overcast as Calvin sped down the freeway toward Visitacion Valley. I suspected the living conditions couldn't be much worse than the first time I'd been in the Bay Area when all I could afford was that windowless studio on Skid Row. He pulled off San Bruno Street onto Arleta Avenue, pointing out the projects where OJ Simpson grew up. The road sloped into a valley leading to his place. It looked like the deed belonged to *Morticia Addams*. Rotted wood siding hung loosely from rusty nails on the dilapidated frame, the windows were cracked, and the front steps were crumbling.

The oldest Section Eight projects were around the corner by the Cow Palace, where Ray had played basketball tournaments in the fifties. But things had changed drastically since then. The valley was impoverished. Gentrification had corralled people of color out of their old neighborhoods and into the district. I must have been the only Caucasian in the borough.

As I grabbed my duffle bags from Calvin's trunk, I saw the torso of a drunkard a few doors down, stretched halfway out his window, yelling incomprehensibly into the wind. Dogs were barking, and a police siren blared in the distance. As I followed Calvin into the house, I could see the inside was as shabby as the exterior, with holes punched in the sheetrock and a leaking roof.

What had I gotten myself into?

A ginormous red Doberman galloped in from the backyard. I dropped my bags as he stopped and growled at my crotch like he wanted to tear my balls off.

"Hey there, Marcus," Calvin said, petting him. "Don't worry, he's super friendly," he assured me.

He'd named the pup after Marcus Garvey, a Jamaican activist who repatriated Liberia. And he was right about the dog who, within minutes, began licking my face and nosing through my bags to see if I'd brought him any treats. He followed us cheerfully as Calvin showed me to my room on the first floor. A casement window overlooking the street swung back and forth against the frame. Each time it slammed shut, it shook the house and startled me, yet I was grateful to have a place to call my own.

After settling in, I rang the personnel agency to see if Mr. Jackson could help me find a job again. He invited me to drop in. But the streets of Visitacion Valley were too dangerous to walk alone to a bus stop, and cabs wouldn't pick you up. When I'd go to the corner store, I had to take Marcus the Doberman for protection. He was as harmless as Marmaduke. But the canine was so humongous that neighbors along the route would jump fences when they saw him, fearful that he might mow them down.

Calvin offered me a ride into town a week later. His jeep came within inches of rear-ending a limousine in front of Mr. Jackson's office building. My friend was so stoned that he didn't even notice. As I exited, Calvin's ganja smoke drifted over to the passengers getting into the limo. A short, mustached man in a three-piece suit waved his hand in front of his nose. I recognized him from the photos on Mr. Jackson's wall.

It was Mayor Willie Brown, and he was frowning at us. In the years that followed, I'd often see him on the cable car or cozying up to a couple of girls at Harry Denton's Starlight Room. The man was so glib. I could never understand what the decent Arthur Jackson, whom I was late to see, liked about him.

Inside the office, I could tell my recruiter's health was failing, but he remained a workaholic. He sent me to a court reporting agency downtown. It was tedious work, but I was thankful for printing and binding depositions all day. From then on, I'd spend most of my time in the financial district, trying to stay out of Calvin's house.

One night, our friendship evaporated after two local radio DJs came by for drugs, and a shouting match erupted. We'd been discussing news about an intifada in the Middle East, and my fair-weather friend decided to take issue with my Judaism.

"Raf, dog. You can't see this straight because you're part of the problem," he said, sitting on the floor, sorting out baggies. "Jews shouldn't even be there—like not even as visitors. There's a reason they call it an *occupation*, bro."

"What are you saying? You think the situation is that cut and dry?" I asked.

I empathized with the Palestinians, but Calvin had denied Israel's right to exist, and he knew it would trigger me. Beneath his aggressive posture, though, was unresolved jealousy over Thalia. She was Jewish, like me, and I hadn't realized she'd broken his heart in college.

I went from being his old pal to a scapegoat overnight.

Not knowing where I would live, I contacted Mr. Jackson in the morning. He knew of a landlord with an available studio on Polk Street right by the California Cable Car line. I left Calvin's that day and signed a twelve-month lease.

It was the postcard picture of San Francisco I'd always envisioned. The trolley bell rang at seven a.m. as it skidded down the tracks, giving me just enough time to throw on some clothes and catch it downtown. All my salary went to rent. But my neighbor was a bartender at the local dive, The Hyde Out, and treated me on weekends to a cocktail or two. I would miss the red Doberman's kisses, but it was safer than living in that wretched valley.

My screenplay, meanwhile, had made the rounds. There were no bites. My agent, who'd promised me the moon, was flummoxed at how fruitless her solicitations had panned out. I was let down, too, but been rejected so many times that I was prepared to put the pen down for good. Mine was not as mighty as the sword, and I needed a new outlet to express myself.

I found it a month before 9/11 in a little building on Fell Street.

* * *

I'd been accepted to the New College School of Law, a San Francisco institution whose alumni included activists like Tom Hayden and Angela Davis. It didn't require a bachelor's degree and was recommended by Bill Coblenz, an attorney I'd met through Mr. Jackson. Bill had established his white-shoe law firm by leveraging access to political allies, including Willie Brown.

In the seventies, he'd successfully represented Patty Hearst, an heiress collared for domestic terrorism. More recently, he'd spearheaded the city's urban renewal strategy, which displaced artists and families, fundamentally changing the city's character.

He was a power broker. And at his firm's 1999 Christmas party at the Marriot Marquis, he approached me over a glass of champagne. We stood together, looking out the tall squeaky-clean windows. Below us, a dozen construction cranes on the horizon turned gracefully like tai chi masters.

"Ever considered law school, Rafael?" he asked me.

"Aren't there enough attorneys?" I replied.

"Enough attorneys. Just not enough capable ones," he remarked, taking a sip from his champagne flute and leaving it on a high top.

I watched him head back toward the banquet room, flanked by a gaggle of junior associates. Bill was an ardent capitalist but, by night, had a seedier side to him, having been rumored to be a longstanding member of the hedonist Bohemian Club. When he learned I'd been accepted at the leftist law school two years later, he applauded it.

At New College, I felt like my real quest in life had begun.

My first course was with Professor Peter Gabel, an erudite scholar responsible for the school's subversive curriculum. He was also the editor of *Tikkun*, a quarterly magazine that aspired to be *The Atlantic*. Peter taught us Contracts, and while we were assigned the standard casebook, there was an additional reading requirement in his class—*The Communist Manifesto* by Karl Marx.

He taught Marx not to juxtapose his ideas with the rule of law in the US but as a viable alternative to our governing model. All classes were based on critical theory and the premise that precedents we studied were systemically flawed and unjust. To Peter, the system needed to be destroyed and rebuilt from the ground up by any means necessary. The campus was swarming with malcontents like him. And I, an idealist who dreamed of making a difference, became one of his useful idiots.

That brainwashing continued into year two when I took Criminal Law, taught by the wife of William Harris, a member of the Symbionese Liberation Army. During her lecture, we were interrupted by news that her husband had been arrested in connection with a cold case, the death of Myrna Lee Opsahl. He'd shot her during the Crocker Bank Robbery of 1975, the same year my brother died. His wife, our teacher, had to excuse herself so she could pick up their kids, left stranded when her *better half* was nabbed while dropping them at school. But more disturbing was that gossip around New College's water cooler that week didn't have anything to do with the crime. It was how law enforcement had the audacity to arrest the killer in front of his children.

I began questioning my decision to attend that school, though I intended to finish. But first, I had to satisfy its internship requirement, so I went back to work at Bill's law firm. Surprisingly, when I applied for the credit, Peter Gabel denied me, claiming it was a for-profit partnership that didn't live up to the school's values. To get his blessing, I would need to work *for free* at a non-profit, making it impossible to get by without going further into debt. It had been awhile since I'd spoken to Eleanor and Ray and been disowned. I couldn't ask them for help and had little choice but to withdraw. Foreseeably, the Western Association of Schools shut New College down three years later.

I kept plugging away at the firm, transitioning into the IT department, learning all I could and picking up pointers that would lead to a rewarding business career. At the time, though, the job felt like a gag prize, one you might win by picking the wrong curtain on *The Price is Right*. I'd spun the big wheel and didn't even get to keep the change, left only with ballooning student debt. But I was independent, maturing in ways I didn't yet fully understand, and just around the corner from facing my monster.

* * *

My love life wasn't as deranged as the New College syllabus but served the same purpose—helping me recognize my unhealthy attraction to extremities.

That compulsion became clear one day after falling for a licentious woman I'd just met on my coffee break. Raised in a small town in Michigan, she'd been in a gruesome accident with a carload of cheerleaders in high school. As the sole survivor, she woke up after a long coma suffering from amnesia. It took a year to recover. The day she renewed her driver's license, she changed the name she'd been given, Polly, to that of the Greek goddess Athena and drove to California.

She was petite but had the loudest, most boisterous laugh ever heard. I couldn't tell if it was natural or her own creation.

After work, we caught the cable car and rode it to The Hyde Out in Nob Hill, drinking until the last call. As I got off the barstool to use the restroom, Athena handed me two quarters, told me to drop them in the jukebox, and to select any song I liked.

I picked Patsy Cline's *Crazy*.

When I came out of the can, she was prancing on the bar counter like a burlesque dancer, belting out the classic ballad. Patrons in the bar jeered as she strode from one end to the other, tipping over glasses. The bartender, my neighbor, demanded we leave. But I should have learned that night that trying to control Athena was futile.

She refused to go until the song was over.

After singing the last line, "I'm crazy for trying and crazy for crying, and I'm crazy for loving you," she jumped off the bar counter into my arms. I fell backward, knocking my head against the wall.

We stumbled out, ambling the length of the marina to the Golden Gate Bridge. As it started drizzling, we ran hand in hand across it until reaching a road leading into Sausalito. It must have been a mile before we arrived at her airstream trailer, sopping wet. She'd parked it behind an abandoned building with half a dozen other Winnebagos. As I stepped inside, I was gobsmacked, glaring at the antiques and books she'd managed to stuff in there. It's like she'd bought out a yard sale.

I watched her change into a pajama shirt. She seemed more awake than she'd been twelve hours earlier when we first hooked up. But I needed sleep, so I removed my shoes, sank into her waterbed, and shut my eyes.

"I'm sorry, but I have to work, handsome," she said, kissing my cheek.

"At four a.m.?" I asked drearily.

"I'm sorry, my love," she replied melodramatically. "I must get to work. But don't worry. I work from home. Ha-ha!"

I struggled to keep my eyes on Athena as we jiggled on her mattress. She put on a headset and dialed into a phone service. I could only hear her voice on the line, so I was spared the heavy breathing on the other end.

She was a sex phone operator!

But I'll admit her vocation was tantalizing, and when she was done, she cuddled up to me and fell asleep on my chest.

She snored as the sun shined through the sliding glass window above us in the morning. When she finally awoke, I tried to persuade her to quit the phone sex gig and get a respectable job. She entertained my appeal but had no intention of doing such a thing. I asked around feverishly and secured her an interview at the law firm.

The following week, one of Bill's associates walked over to my cubicle and told me she wasn't fit for the position.

"Raf, I'll be honest. This girl you sent. She's—well, she's too *talented* for the job. You need to let her pursue her other passions," he said.

"I don't think you know her passions," I replied.

"I have *some* idea," the young lawyer said coyly. "Let me make it up to you. I've got a couple of extra tickets to the theater this weekend. She's an actress, right? She'll love it."

"Thanks," I responded, agreeing to pick up the tickets at will call.

When Saturday came, Athena showed up at my apartment dressed like she was attending the Academy Awards—of 1929. We made it to the theater moments before the curtain came up. It was a snobby Noël Coward play, and the audience was madly in love with every line. Their laughter was like a metronome, a regimented wave of guffaws that sounded more programmed than a laugh track. But while I thought the jokes sucked, Athena loved them. The only problem was the three-second pause between the audience laughing and her getting the punchline.

Her delayed laughter was bearable at first. But by the second act, it became a distraction. Heads began to turn, and there was snickering. I tried to pinch Athena, hoping she'd pipe down, but she just continued laughing like a hyena. Even the actors on stage became distracted, and their timing was thrown off. Then the audience ceased laughing entirely. But even that didn't stop Athena.

She kept laughing. And laughing. And laughing.

We were escorted out and confronted by the manager in the lobby.

"Madam, this cannot continue," he warned my date.

"What cannot continue, sir?" Athena asked sincerely.

"Making a mockery of this play, madam."

"A mockery?"

"With the laughing, madam. *The laughing,*" he said, adjusting his big red tie.

"A mockery of this right here?" she asked, waving the playbill.

"Yes, madam, and I shall remind you—"

But Athena had enough of him by that point and got in his face vociferously.

"No, sir. I shall remind you! It's a comedy! You're supposed to laugh!"

She took me by the arm and we began to jet, but just as I cracked the door for her, Athena spun around to give the man one last piece of her mind.

"And if I may," she said, looking him over, "lose the tie. It makes you look like a fucking circus clown."

She was a crazy, erratic nymph, as unpredictable intimately as she was publicly in the bars and theaters where I accompanied her. The artist in me thought I'd found my muse and didn't want to let her go. With time, my adoration began to fade.

Our last day together was three months later at the Standard Hotel in Los Angeles. I was taking a meeting with a new literary agent. Sitting by the pool, Athena appeared bored. She started flirting with a young, tattooed waiter and stepped away. I was too involved in my conversation to notice her absence. After lunch, I went looking for her.

As I searched the lobby, I discovered her—in a large glass case behind the concierge desk, stripped down to her skivvies and crawling around like a tiger. It was a feature of the hotel brand back then. Athena smiled and waved at me before kissing the glass and leaving a mark on it with her big strawberry lips.

She'd found a new home, and it was over between us.

And though I'd grown used to getting hit with surprises like that, nothing could prepare me for the next curveball.

Rebirths

In 1977, more than a million unwanted pregnancies in the United States resulted in abortion. I got lucky, carried to term, and given up for adoption. The arrangement should have been routine, except that my birth mother was the troubled daughter of a prolific film composer and an acclaimed singer. Any disclosure of her circumstances might have caused a scandal and, in their view, disgraced the family. Afraid of repercussions, they took extraordinary measures to keep everything under wraps.

So did my adopted family.

I only discovered their collusion by accident thirty years later.

It had been seven years since I'd spoken to Eleanor and Ray. I regarded them with contempt, having pinned the guilt for my unrealized dreams on our strained kinship. My resentment was inordinate, but they'd hidden a big secret from me. In that darkness, I couldn't see that the crux of my insecurities and my inability to maintain meaningful relationships was entwined with a festering fear of abandonment.

It was also the perfect disguise for the monster lurking within me.

Then, one night, something extraordinary happened as I sat alone by my bay window. I began to see the world as it was rather than how I wished it would be.

I could no longer pretend the past was in black and white.

* * *

I'd picked up a magazine in the hotel lobby during my last visit to Los Angeles. It featured an article about Louise Brown, the first test-tube baby. She was pictured cutting a big yellow ribbon at a supermarket opening in Lancashire, England, surrounded by jolly grocery workers. The write-up piqued my curiosity when it noted the woman's birthdate as July 25th, 1978. And why was this relevant? Because my parents had told me that I, too, was a test-tube baby—born *seventeen months before Louise.*

"You're a test-tube baby" was the elaborate ruse Mom and Dad devised to conceal their secret as I grew more curious about our age gap. They first floated the idea a few days after we'd met the Osbournes, who'd presumed I was Eleanor's grandson. Louise's birth was big news in the 1970s, and Mom figured that since the girl's birthday was close to mine, it might be easy to conflate. She cajoled me into believing I was born in the same manner and not to discuss it, insisting it was "experimental" and "hush-hush."

But why did everybody else in my life go along with it?

Because Eleanor was the matriarch, the lioness on our coat of arms, and had sworn everyone to secrecy. Like a mafia don, nobody dared cross her. My father and sisters also loved her too much to breach her trust. Uncles, aunts, cousins, and family friends like the Landons, Sterlings, and Gilberts kept her secret and sang the tune. For years, her lie held up against my sporadic attempts to deconstruct it.

At some point, I gave up trying.

Then, that evening, when it was about the furthest thing from my mind, I accidentally came across Louise's birthdate, and Eleanor's tangled web came undone.

I began re-examining our physical differences. The Moscatels were of Turkish descent and darker than me, with no freckles—not one. In our living room, a framed ancestral photo from Istanbul sat on the baby grand. The older men in the picture wore fezzes.

That type of hat wouldn't look right on me, I thought, *unless I became a Shriner.*

There were no blue eyes in the family either, just mine. And my father, Ray, was a towering hulk whose athletic prowess I'd somehow failed to inherit. The layers of fabrication I peeled back were as abrasive as wet sand in a swimsuit.

I called Dad with the news I'd read about Louise. He regurgitated the test-tube story but had recently fallen off the wagon, and his recollection was sloppy. As the discrepancies piled up, Dad went for the Hail Mary.

"It was all done under the table, son. You have to understand that test-tube babies were a very, uh, new thing in those days."

"That right?" I said, listening incredulously.

"We were told not to say anything," he added.

"Not to say anything?"

"No. Not a word. Didn't want the doctors to get in trouble," he said, clearing his throat.

I'd heard the explanation before but could no longer believe it.

Mom caught wind of his *babajadas* on the phone. It's a Ladino word that translates to "babbling." Cutting in on our conversation, she vehemently denied everything. She countered my claims with grandiose affirmations, infuriated that I would dare question her motives. Yet her energetic rebuttals could no longer squelch my curiosity. As she raised her voice, my mind began to consider that much of my life was pure fiction, based on a forgery. It wasn't malicious falsification but a fraud, nonetheless.

I hung up and decided to get to the bottom of it. After all, how could I know where I was going if I never knew where I'd been? Somewhere on the planet, maybe spinning pies in a Bronx pizzeria or plowing a hay field in Sweden, were a bunch of people that walked and talked just like me. Where were these people—*my people*? And which of them had the bright idea to leave me on Eleanor Moscatel's doorstep?

***

Reeling from the discovery, I requested my birth records from the State of California. Eight weeks later, on the day before Thanksgiving, a sealed manila envelope arrived. Inside, fastened with a rusty paper clip, was a stack of medical records and handwritten notes from a social worker that would turn my world upside down.

The first document was titled *Circumstances of Placement* and read:

> Your birth mother made the decision to place you for adoption because she felt it was best for you. She wanted to pursue her career and believed a child needed a two-parent home. She also felt she wasn't ready for parenthood. Your adoption was arranged by her physician and an attorney. You were placed in your adoptive family's home on March 13, 1977.

Those words were jarring but not as much as those that followed:

> Your birth mother and your birth father, who was married, met one another at a bar and began seeing one another. Your birth father told your birth mother that he loved both her and his wife. She stated that she knew the relationship had no future. However, she believed you were conceived out of love, and she suspected that subconsciously she may have wanted a child so as to hold on to your birth father. She wrote to your birth father when she learned that she was pregnant

> but did not hear back from him. She believed that he might have been shocked as his wife was also expecting a child.

A few pages behind those notes was the hospital discharge summary:

> This young lady was admitted for normal delivery. She went through an emotional crisis since the baby was going out for adoption.

"She went through an emotional crisis," I repeated to myself.

Those six words scribbled in cursive softened the blow of my abandonment, lending some context to the lurid circumstances. But it would be months before I connected the rest of the dots. Shuffling downstairs to the bodega on the first floor of my apartment complex, I bought a case of Peroni.

I had questions.

Who was I? Was I even Jewish? What about my long-held interests in religion, literature, and Lakers basketball? How much of me was nature, and how much was nurture? Was I walking in my true ancestor's footsteps, or had I blindly modeled myself after the Moscatels because they'd taken me in?

Most importantly, why on earth was my name Rafael? I looked nothing like a Rafael! And nobody could ever pronounce it right. I was maybe a Jim, a Fred, a Tim, or even a Bucky. But *Rafael*?

My parents had a lot of explaining to do.

I hadn't planned to spend the holidays in Los Angeles, but I grabbed the manila envelope and flew in to square it up with Eleanor and Ray. We sat in the wicker chairs on the checkered patio that afternoon, where Morticia's Peacock chair still gathered dust. Mom came clean with everything she knew. Her deceit riled me. Yet as tears streamed from my eyes and down my cheeks, I realized that somehow, I had to find a way to absolve her, as she had forgiven me countless times.

The terrible secret she'd kept was painful, but my love for Eleanor, borne over a lifetime of her being there for me, could heal any wound.

"Why didn't you just tell me, Mom?" I asked, shaking my head.

"I didn't think you would love us anymore," she admitted. "I thought you would leave us to go be with your other family and mother."

"This *is* my family," I asserted as we embraced. "And *you* are my mother."

Eleanor's actions may seem self-serving. But she'd lost her beloved son two short years before I was adopted and vowed never to lose a child again. Tearful, she described the day her close friend, Miss Dottie, approached my birth mother. The woman had been tossed out of her mom's New York condo and had moved in with her controlling father in Bel Air. The man would tolerate his daughter's pregnancy insofar as she could find a way to get rid of it, and abortion was an option she'd been seriously considering.

When Don Sterling became aware of the predicament, he offered to approach my birth mother on Eleanor's behalf with a lucrative offer. The Moscatel family would financially support the woman if she agreed to hand me over upon birth. And Don would do everything in his power to seal the records so they would never see the light of day.

After Albert was killed, he watched Eleanor battle anxiety and depression for months. And as thoughtless as the man could sometimes be, her suffering broke his heart. He couldn't bear seeing the same exuberant woman who'd burst into his office years before so downcast. He had his own adopted children and told Eleanor that taking me in would help things.

I could almost hear his voice coming through the notes I'd read in the adoption file, whispering into my birth mother's ear, "Sweetheart, you know this baby was conceived out of love. You don't want to terminate the pregnancy. Let's take care of it another way. We'll make it easy."

I'll never know exactly how Don convinced her to give me up. It doesn't matter in the grand scheme of things. I'm just thankful he was there for Mom when she needed him most.

It was Donald T. Sterling, *the absolute last soul on earth you'd ever trust to watch out for a kid like me,* who saved my life.

* * *

Don was running a busy personal injury practice the year I was adopted. It had been long since then, and I didn't expect he'd recollect much from those days, but he couldn't be bothered. He wouldn't even take my call, delegating his secretary to respond rather curtly, "he doesn't know anything!" I questioned whether he was hiding behind attorney-client privilege, which was improbable based on our family history, or if it had something to do with his son.

I racked my brain, trying to piece together the puzzle. It reminded me of the treasure maps Scotty and I drew as kids. How hard could it be to track down and dig up this locked chest of secrets? Were there clues at the foot of that rocky cove where we'd played as children?

Undeterred, I decided I didn't need or want Don's help and would find the truth alone. But the remaining papers in the adoption file weren't useful. The doctors' names and those of my biological family had all been redacted. Still, the notes in the file gave me a window into the inner workings of a family more concerned with their careers and reputations than taking personal responsibility.

According to the state's records, I was conceived in the Big Apple. My birth mother was a five-foot-three Ashkenazi, produced radio commercials, and was an aspiring songwriter. My biological father was German, short, blond, and an undercover narcotics officer for the NYPD. That's all I had to go on.

Discouraged, I asked Eleanor if she could recall anything else about the adoption. She erroneously thought the family's last name was "Kizzy." So, I wasted weeks sending letters to people with that surname in upstate New York, none of whom I was actually related to.

Over the next six months, I spent thousands on sleuths who promised they could track down my relatives. I couldn't afford to pay them all, but luckily my oldest sister, Laurie, footed some of the bills. She may have felt bad having to keep the secret from me. Yet none of the investigators could get further than what was already in the adoption file. By the fourth of July, I was ready to throw in the towel. Then, that night, as fireworks exploded above the Golden Gate Bridge, I caught a break.

I'd stayed home and was flipping through cable channels when I stumbled on a documentary about Darryl McDaniels of Run-DMC. Like me, the rapper discovered late in life that he was adopted. It resulted in a heartwarming reconciliation with his birth mother. In McDaniels, I found renewed hope for my search. I contacted Pamela Slayton, the investigator he'd hired. I had names, phone numbers, and addresses in less than a day.

***

Pamela called me with her findings as I arrived home from work. She recommended that I sit down and take some deep breaths.

"You're not going to believe this, Rafael."

I fell into my leather chaise and looked out the bay window where I'd first cracked the case of Louise Brown, which led to this moment.

She strung together the next few words like I was on *This Is Your Life*.

"You come from an interesting family of singers and musicians," she said.

I'd always assumed most adoptees were a by-product of abject poverty or a single parent unable to support and nurture their child. It was hardly my scenario. The clan that dropped me at the pound was a wildly successful family of entertainers. They were quite capable of taking care of a child born out of wedlock in the spring of 1977.

They chose not to.

"Your grandfather is named Vic Mizzy," Pamela explained with cadence. "He's alive. Lives in Bel Air. It's something. He wrote the music for TV shows like, well, you might have heard of these even though they're before your time—*Green Acres* or *The Addams Family?*"

"Oh, whoa. Yeah, I used to watch Herman and Eddie and all those characters when I was a kid," I recalled.

Baffled by the revelation, I'd mixed up the theme song to *The Addams Family* with *The Munsters,* so Pamela attempted to hum the right notes.

"No, no, it's the one that goes 'buh-dah-dah-dum, click-click, buh-dah-dah-dum, click-click.'"

Immediately I recognized it, although I'd associated the melody with shot clock music at the LA Clippers games I'd attended with Scotty.

"Wow," I replied, dumbfounded.

It was the kookiest detail because Mom and Dad had purchased our home on Beverly Drive from actress Carolyn Jones. She played *Morticia Addams* on the hit show. Vic Mizzy must have known the woman somewhat well, having written the music for each episode and coached her in the sitcom's opening credits.

What were the chances? I wondered, thinking of that old Peacock chair that had sat on our patio since I was born.

Then her voice grew melancholy.

"I also have some bad news, kid."

An adoptee herself, Pamela's own experience hadn't gone smoothly. She broke it to me the way only a child who endured a similar outcome could.

"Your biological mother, Patty Lou. She—she passed in 1995. March 12th."

It was the day after my eighteenth birthday.

"I'm sorry, kid," Pamela said, giving me time to process it.

The date hit me like a freight train, a grim realization that I'd never meet Patty, get to know what kind of person she was, or even ask about what happened to *us*. She'd died from toxic shock syndrome, possibly caused by tuberculosis. They buried her in Mount Lebanon Cemetery in Queens County, New York, and published her obituary in *Variety*. She was forty-nine.

"You want more?" she asked, anticipating my response.

"Yes, everything you've got, please."

I could hear her shuffling some papers on the other end of the line.

"Your grandmother, her name is Mary Small. I guess she was a popular singer in her day. She's still alive. Living in New York, but I couldn't find an address. Your mother also had a sister—"

"Wait. What about my birth father?"

She hesitated. "I found him too. He's in Florida. Do you want his address?"

"Yes."

Pamela then warned me against having high hopes for reuniting with the family. In many cases, she expounded, it didn't work out nicely as it had for McDaniels. But I wasn't afraid. I had to know from where I'd come to figure out where I was destined to go.

***

Since my mother was dead, I wrote to my birth father. He'd left his first wife to start a new family in Miami. He mailed me a one-paragraph note in my handwriting, reporting he was in good health and asking that I not pursue a relationship. I honored the request but knew he was a man I could never respect. As an undercover cop in 1970s New York, I bet he had some heroic stories. Running around behind his wife's back while she was pregnant probably wasn't one of them.

Next, I wrote to my aunt, hoping she'd be more sensitive and receptive. Her reply was scathing, a passive-aggressive screed deriding her sister, my birth mother, and requesting that I not contact their father, the frail Vic Mizzy. It was a shrill piece of prose intended to encumber me. She'd claimed others had purported to be Vic's grandson and attempted to extort him. I was insulted by her wild inference that I was after his estate.

All I wanted was the truth.

Ironically, while sifting through publicity photos in the composer's archives one weekend, I realized we'd once met at the Beverly Hills Hotel. I'd stop by whenever I was passing through town. It was Vic's stomping ground too. In 1964 he'd accidentally knocked heads in their pool with a television producer. That chance encounter would lead to him scoring *The Addams Family*. Because of his fondness for the hotel, he continued to frequent it.

The night we crossed paths, my date and I sat at the Polo Lounge, enjoying a Ramos Fizz. While bantering with the bartender, he pointed out a few of Tinseltown's greats packed into a green booth behind us. In the middle sat comedian Red Buttons. He was beside a man who, in retrospect, looked like I might in fifty years.

I coaxed my date, a youthful girl with an hourglass figure, into introducing herself to the dinner party. Clasping her rhinestone purse, she sashayed over to them and delivered a line I'd composed.

"Mr. Buttons. I wish I had words to pay you the compliment you deserve, but you've taken my breath away," she said with a big Texas smile.

It was schmaltzy, and Buttons ate it up like the other old-timers in the booth. They shamelessly flirted with her until I dragged her away. But before departing, I remember Vic looking straight at me for a few seconds. I didn't understand the significance of that encounter and hadn't thought about it since.

Ignoring my aunt's warnings, I remained hopeful for a reunion.

Surely, my own grandfather wouldn't reject me? I thought.

But even Pamela couldn't get Vic's phone number, so I could only write him letters that came back "return to sender."

Then, seeing how much her lie had affected me, Eleanor decided to do what she could to help. She learned Vic would be signing copies of his latest album at a record store in Hollywood. I was stuck in San Francisco, so she offered to go and speak to him for me. It was ninety-plus degrees that day, and my aging parents waited in line an hour before reaching his table.

"Vic," my mother said with trepidation.

"Yeeessss," he replied, thinking she was a longtime fan.

"I'm Eleanor. And this is Ray, my husband. I don't know how to say this, but a very long time ago, we adopted your grandson."

Vic dropped his pen and leaned back, speechless.

"I know it's quite a surprise," Mom said, handing him a recent photo of me.

"You must be mistaken. I don't have a—Who are you, again?"

Eleanor explained. He was confounded as if he'd made some deal with the devil, and payment was due. He thanked Mom for coming, indicating he'd contact me after the signing.

The call never came.

My mother consoled me, but I felt worse for Vic. He'd lost a daughter and now a grandson. Eleanor didn't give up on trying to help, though. She looked through her storage and dug up a notarized agreement she'd found in an old shoebox. It was on Don Sterling's letterhead, documenting a loan to my birth mother, which read:

> I, Patricia Lou Mizzy, hereby acknowledge receipt of five hundred dollars. Said amount will be repaid by me upon receipt of payment of monies due me for reimbursement.

It seemed peculiar that Patty had to borrow money. Her father, Vic, was a big shot in Hollywood, a musical prodigy who'd earned a fortune producing a substantial body of work. That's why his stinginess in supporting his daughter through her pregnancy was all the more disappointing. I gave up any further attempts to meet him, and he died alone in his Bel Air mansion a few months later.

Pamela, my investigator, had been right all along. I should have set expectations low. It turns out I had more luck being placed in the proverbial basket of reeds and sent down the river, like Moses. My birth father was an unfaithful cad, and my birth mother could barely raise herself. Life with the Moscatels, in comparison, was a Shangri-la. They weren't perfect, but they loved, cared for, and forgave me. It was now time for me to accept and forgive them. I started thinking about moving back home for good. My days as a prodigal son were numbered.

One last stone was left unturned, however.

A social worker in New York had left me a text message replying to an inquiry I'd made months earlier. He'd broken protocol to alert me that my grandmother Mary Small was in her eleventh hour in a Harlem hospice.

Her dying wish was to see me.

* * *

It couldn't have come at a more difficult time. I'd been trying to put my whole adoption in the rearview, but it wasn't quite through with me. I'd still never touched the skin of a single person with whom I shared DNA. And since retaining Pamela to help me find my birth family, Mary was always in the back of my mind.

I took a taxi to LAX. Seven hours later, I was in Gotham.

The subway dropped me close to Harlem General on Malcolm X

Boulevard. I walked the rest of the way. Checking in at the nurse's station, I was informed that I was the only person to have visited the dying starlet. Mary had spent her entire nest egg on healthcare in her final years and was too proud to let friends see her enfeebled, which is just one reason nobody dropped by. Her husband Vic and the rest of the family had written her off.

For some reason, she asked to see me, the grandson she never knew.

I stepped into the dimly lit room, a bundle of nerves, and pulled a chair next to her gurney. There she was, the only blood relative I'd ever get to know, aside from my future children. Carefully, I unlocked the bedrail so I could lean over.

Moving closer, I said, "Mary. It's me. Patty's son. Rafael," and gently kissed her cheek.

I don't know if she wanted the kiss, but it's what I would have. She smiled with her remaining strength and closed her eyes.

When Mary Small learned Patty was impregnated by the married cop she'd been fooling around with, she went ballistic. Being old-fashioned, she kicked her daughter out and never spoke to her again. Sitting with her withered body in that frigid room that afternoon, I knew something about their volatile relationship from my aunt's letter. I was conflicted and upset that Mary had thrown my birth mother out. But the Moscatels taught me to respect elders, whatever their failings, so I came to be with her.

It's not easy to forgive—especially these days in a society obsessed with presentism and castigating past mistakes. Whether you're a private person or a public persona, the slightest error can get you canceled, forgotten, and erased from history, even when it's family. It feels like there's no context anymore. It's all judgment.

I didn't want to discard Mary, Patty, or Eleanor because of their lies or shortcomings. I left the hospital that day, reminding myself that everybody screws up and we all have our monsters.

When my plane landed back at LAX, Mary's social worker had left a voicemail saying she was gone. My gut says she held on living for me, and before she died, as her lips mustered that smile, she seemed relieved to know the child carried by her daughter had turned out okay.

That's when I realized that not only do we all have our monsters but they could be defeated. Some just take longer to eradicate than others. They may not be the stuff of epic myths like Beowulf or Gilgamesh. And they can't be erased simply by closing the book, turning the page, or telling ourselves a lie.

They must be dealt with.

Even the ugliest can be vanquished, but only when we shine the light in their eyes, unafraid to face our own reflection.

The truth of my adoption, letdowns and all, had set me free. A dam had burst, and tears I'd held back flooded into the smoldering valley below, extinguishing embers along the banks of the meandering river that had been my life. It had been ablaze since my birth mother forsook me. I'd been burned yet survived. All that was left was the story of the little monster I once was and the promise of the man I had another chance to become.

* * *

My identity crisis was resolved, and my sense of belonging was restored, but matters of trust remained. Every romantic relationship I'd pursued had felt more critical and dramatic than the last. I was almost too careful not to hurt my lovers or waste their time. I didn't want to waste mine, either. Being thirty, I'd sown my oats and needed someone I could be with forever. But since I traveled for work, I never pictured finding a stable partner as I was usually in an airport terminal. And yet, that's precisely where I was when I saw the most effervescent woman I'd ever meet—Abby.

She was flying back from a conference and checking the departure screen. I was seated across from her at a restaurant. At first glance, I raised my pint glass, just as Dad had to Mom back in Seattle when they met. She picked up her hobo bag, walked over, and asked if the seat next to me had been taken.

"Whatcha writing?" she asked, noticing my laptop.

It could have been the first draft of this book, but I can't remember.

The scenery around us fell away like a time-lapse video, travelers disappearing into thin air, the airport announcements fading to white noise. Everything except Abby was gone instantly as if it had never existed. We chatted until our flight started boarding but learned it was overbooked as we arrived at the gate. I began worrying about falling behind on the IT work waiting for me at the law firm in San Francisco. But then, as she smiled, I realized that *I was the person waiting*—for the one standing right in front of me.

Abby was more down to earth than the women I'd known. Raised on a family farm in central Ohio, her mother taught special needs, and her father was a devoted husband. She seemed to accept me the way Kris had, without pretense. And while the girl had drunk some of the same Kool-Aid I had at college, she wasn't jaded. Like my mother, she was a late bloomer, had gotten most of her act together, and decided the only direction she would move was forward.

We caught a later plane to Oakland. I'd planned to take the subway to my place in San Francisco but didn't return to my apartment that night. Instead, I spent it with Abby, sitting on a park bench by Lake Merritt. We yammered until sunrise as joggers began to circle the dirt trail along the shoreline. One, an older man, was running at a slower pace. He looked familiar—like he'd once left an oil stain on my mother's driveway.

"Do you know that guy?" Abby asked, her head resting on my shoulder.

I could tell it was Jerry Brown, now the mayor of Oakland. But I didn't want to ruin the moment.

"Never seen him before in my life," I said, bringing her close and kissing her.

* * *

From that day, Abby and I were inseparable. We spent evenings gallivanting around San Francisco, dancing until dawn at the Tonga Room, bar crawling in North Beach, and making out at the Top of the Mark. We were young, insatiable, and made for each other. But a few months later, it was time to return to LA and be closer to my parents.

As soon as I'd settled in, Abby came for a visit. I picked her up at the airport where we'd met three months prior. I thought she was *the one*. But she hadn't lived with a man, and moving in with one she barely knew was a huge step. We'd never fought, yet we began arguing that day like an old couple about something trivial. I tried to calm her down, but the conflict escalated as we approached Cañon Drive, where I'd once waited for my bus as a teenager.

Up ahead in the road, an older man in a trench coat and sunglasses was in the crosswalk. I was so steeped in my argument with Abby that I almost didn't react in time to hit the brakes. The car came to a screeching stop, inches from the pedestrian, who jumped like a cat and was nearly killed. He glared at us through the windshield, traumatized.

"That guy looks famous," Abby said quietly.

My hands shook as they gripped the wheel.

"It's Al Pacino," I replied with my teeth clenched, recognizing the actor from my favorite movie, *The Godfather*.

We waved at him like a couple of bubbleheaded tourists as he stepped onto the curb, leering at us. In our nervous laughter, we forgot the argument by the next block. But I can guarantee that if we'd run over

Al Pacino that day, there's no way we'd have been married.

My wife was Christian, and I was Jewish, so we chose a Buddhist Rinban to join us in holy matrimony. He conducted our ceremony on a yacht in Marina del Rey, where long ago, I'd saved my parents and their friends from drowning at sea. Eleanor and Ray sat beside one another, just like back then, buoyant.

When I put the ring on Abby's finger, I believed she was my soulmate. But my greatest obstacle lay ahead—one that would either destroy the monster or me.

* * *

A year after the wedding, I was hired by an executive at Paramount Pictures. She was an enigmatic, mature brunette, a guarded woman whom most people knew very little. Her reputation in the business was one of a tough negotiator and a vigilant defender of the brand. Some saw her as implacable, others as merciful, but nothing in between. She kept me waiting an hour in the reception area before our first meeting. I sat anxiously in my new navy suit, listening to the clock tick.

On the wall was the poster for *The Graduate,* which felt serendipitous because, in 1967, Mom had her legs sketched for it. The advertisement turned out to be as noteworthy as the film. Another actress has claimed it was her gams and may have also modeled for it. But while that lady has reportedly told many fibs, the only lie I ever caught Mom in was when she emphatically denied I was adopted. So as far as I'm concerned, Eleanor Moscatel is the original Mrs. Robinson.

And Mom wasn't the only person I knew who'd worked on the lot. My estranged grandfather, Vic Mizzy, had scored features there, and Michael Landon's son, Christopher, wrote scripts for them. Sadly, it's also where my parents were the night they learned Albert had been hit by a car and died. Still, I didn't want to tell my interviewer about those connections that afternoon. I wanted her to see me for who I was.

Her door opened automatically.

"Go ahead," motioned the assistant.

With my resume in hand, I entered her modern office, sparsely decorated with glass-blown paperweights and one framed picture on her desk.

"Please, have a seat," she said, signing some paperwork.

I sat on her suede divan by a window overlooking a courtyard. Outside, the hallowed administration building adjoined the studio's iconic arched gate. The woman stood and walked toward me methodically. Sitting in a Barcelona chair, she crossed her legs and picked up a legal pad from the glass table separating us. Right away, we were assessing one another, and despite our ages, there was an unspoken attraction—nothing overtly sexual but pleasant in its subtlety.

"Would you like some water?"

"No, I'm okay, thank you," I replied, showing her a bottle the assistant had given me.

She let me gab for a bit about my work experience. And as much as I swore I would hold back, I couldn't help but slip into a tangent about my grandmother Mary Small. At that moment, the interview could have gone south, with her perceiving me as an opportunist trying to break into the business. But her ears perked up when I mentioned my adoption in the context of visiting my grandmother on her deathbed.

"Oh, that's interesting. I adopted a little girl, myself," she said, smiling toward the single frame on her desk—a black and white photo of a cute Asian toddler.

"Really? How did that happen?" I asked.

"Somebody left her on my doorstep in a basket," she said unflinchingly.

I picked up on her appetite for evasiveness and took it as a sign not to probe. For all I know, the woman opened her front door one day and found a Chinese baby. What did it matter? The same sort of thing happened to me.

I knew she would offer me the position, seeing in me a reflection of her daughter. She liked that I inquired but kept it at arm's length. Within weeks, I'd have an office down the hall at a salary exceeding my asking. I was appreciative. Abby had graduated from law school that past June, and there were bills to pay.

The next few years at Paramount brought prosperity but would come at a price.

* * *

The first thing my new boss tasked me with came a week into the job. I was told to show up at the Burbank airport at ten a.m. and ask for Benicia. The trip was confidential, and nobody explained what I'd be doing or where I'd be flying. I packed a few changes of clothes and arrived early. Benicia was sitting by herself in the terminal, rifling through paperwork.

"Hello," I said, looking down at her.

She was overweight but winsome, with olive skin and fake eyelashes.

"You must be Rafee-el," she replied, judging my suit and crew cut.

"Yes, I work for—"

"I know who you work for."

She was HR and reported to my boss whenever the studio terminated employees.

"Do you understand why you're here?" she asked, jotting down notes and checking boxes on a form.

"I was just told to show up."

"Uh-huh. Okay," Benicia said, pointing her pencil at a rotund gentleman reading the trades. "You know who that is?"

"No."

"That's Walter. One of our chiefs."

Wet behind the ears, I didn't think to acquaint myself with senior management. I'd heard about Brad Grey, the head honcho, but didn't understand Walter's span of control. He was top brass. Looking at me like he smelled something, he crossed over and introduced himself but didn't say much else.

The studio had decided to shutter a subsidiary in Seattle, and I was along to help him do the dirty work. Within minutes of arriving at the satellite office, Walter had fired everybody unable to relocate to California. Benicia instructed me to scour their offices, collecting keys and records as former employees cleaned out their desks.

When the layoff was done, Walter asked if anybody wanted to join him for dinner. I was the only junior executive to accept his invitation. A town car shuttled us to a seafood restaurant on the pier. I was almost dizzy at the table, realizing I'd gone from making cappuccinos for fake power players to dining with real ones.

We were joined by a shipbuilder who'd designed Walter's sailboat, our stodgy Chief Financial Officer, and a few other executives. I felt out of my league on some level, but by happenstance, the shipbuilder knew my uncle, a prominent real estate developer in Seattle. As he expressed his admiration for the Moscatels, the brass started to see me in a different light.

Halfway through dinner, Walter brought up *The Godfather*, produced by Paramount, and the conversation turned to film. I'd purchased it on VHS back in the eighties and had memorized every line. The Chief Financial Officer and I ended up sparring over quotes from the movie, and he became peeved when he realized I knew the story better than him. The man took himself so seriously that he didn't even find it funny when I told him I'd almost run over Michael Corleone!

In the end, it didn't matter. I'd won over the rest of the party, including Walter.

***

I came home invigorated and more seasoned. Executives began inviting me to lunches and asking for my take on projects outside my wheelhouse. I even joined the triathlon team and thought about quitting smoking. The studio's prospects, however, weren't rosy. They were undergoing a restructuring and toying with the idea of a merger. Everybody was skittish about the future, including creatives.

Christopher Landon had a film on that year's slate. I'd never discussed our relationship at work, but colleagues had seen us chatting, and our family history wasn't a secret. By the time he'd made it to Paramount, it was on his merit rather than his father Michael's name. He was a clever writer and had proven himself with the *Paranormal Activity* franchise. Now the studio was allowing him to develop his own material, and he was proud of his new movie.

I'd recently congratulated him when I ran into Walter on the Paseo, a cobblestone walkway behind Paramount's gates. Christopher didn't know it yet, but Paramount was about to slash his film's publicity and advertising budget. They often did that when a movie didn't look like a hit, which wasn't uncommon. But I couldn't believe Walter would divulge it. Either he didn't care or was testing me.

Left in the thorny position of letting Christopher in on it or keeping the decision close to the vest, I chose the latter. I had a job to do at Paramount regardless of our friendship, which wasn't nearly as close as Michael and Dad's.

I kept my head down and worked hard to soak in as much of the business as possible. I made blunders, which limited my advancement, but the steady income helped me shore up my finances and purchase a home with Abby. Still, the daily pressure was intense. My wife and I quarreled. I became absent and unloving, and Abby was the same. We were pursuing our careers instead of planning for our family. I blamed her when I lost promotions and spent more time at the studio than necessary. She hid behind billable hours at her firm, coming home late without good cause until the pregnancy limited her movement. When the baby finally arrived, we weren't prepared for how it would change our lives.

And then Scotty Sterling died, which brings us back to where we began this story.

Amid my grief and marital troubles, Abby and I signed up for counseling. I'd quit smoking after the funeral, which was good for my physical health but made me irritable. Our arguments worsened. After a blowup in our psychologist's office, he advised that we be seen separately. Once he had me alone, he let on that Abby didn't love me at all—that she pitied me from the moment we met.

I was rankled and called my wife from the car.

"Not the first time I've been lied to, Abby!" I shouted into the phone.

"Rafie, that's untrue. I swear I would never say that. Never!"

"You might never say it, but you thought it!"

"Never. Never!" Abby insisted.

I wanted to believe her, but I was still processing my adoption. It was hard to trust anybody between those scars and much of what my parents had modeled for me. We tried to move past it, but our friction was exacerbated with each additional counseling session.

* * *

That summer, not long after his son Scotty died, what was left of Don Sterling's life fell to pieces. Following a leak of lewd comments secretly recorded by his mistress, he became the focal point of media scrutiny and, almost overnight, a pariah. The tape led to his expulsion from the NBA. It was shocking. I knew he was crass but had never heard him talk quite like that.

After Don's remarks began appearing on cable news chyrons, his wife dropped by Eleanor's house, dejected and caught in the crossfire. I happened to be around because I'd been asking Mom's advice about my trouble with Abby.

"Maybe he should just apologize," I suggested to Mrs. Sterling, pouring her a diet soda as she sobbed in our living room.

But Uncle Don wasn't used to being told what to do, let alone what to say. He wouldn't accept responsibility. I wasn't sorry for the man with whom my life had been so entangled. Still, I felt for his family, hounded mercilessly by reporters and humiliated.

Don remained indignant for months, fighting a 21st-century public relations crisis with a 20th-century mindset. He believed he could still take cover from the fallout behind a pair of shades and might have prevailed had he litigated. But ironically, the rushed sale of the team, designed to let the league save face with the players' union, gave Don the upper hand in negotiations. In the end, he walked away with a record-breaking two-billion-dollar windfall.

* * *

I didn't pay much more attention to what happened to Donald T. Sterling after that. I was busy with work and had grown close to Katie, a colleague at the studio. We'd met while training for the triathlon team and often jogged an extra half-mile to get more acquainted. She was tall, with runway legs and a pretty face framed with a wedge cut. Like my wife, she was a transplant from the Midwest—polite, sensible, and motivated. And the woman didn't pity me the way I suspected Abby did. She built up my confidence, drawing me near to her.

As Christmas approached, I thought I'd fallen in love.

That December, she invited Abby and me to a swanky party at the home of a television executive. Walter was camped out on a black satin couch in the sitting room. I shook his hand and sat down beside him. Katie and Abby snuck away to use the restroom, leaving us alone for a minute. I was curious about what he thought of the news that our biggest shareholder was planning a merger.

"What do you think's going to happen to Paramount?" I asked.

"Not sure what you mean, Rafael," he responded, waving to a friend who was leaving.

"I mean, who's going to run the new company?"

"Are you sure that's the plan?" he asked with a smile.

"It's in the paper," I reported.

"Look, Rafael. In business, you sometimes pit one player against another, okay? But you never let on which one you favor. That's the strategy here. What do you expect them to do?"

"Compete?" I answered, following his logic.

"Right. And no matter who outperforms, you win. So does the stock."

I questioned whether I was playing the same game with Abby and Katie.

* * *

When spring came, more rumors were floating around about Paramount's troubles. People started jumping ship. Abby pleaded with me to look for a job that would be less strenuous for our marriage.

I refused, insisting that the studio supported my career. It was partly true, and they sent me to Manhattan that April to speak at a conference. I stayed with my sister Marleigh, who'd moved to nearby Westchester years earlier after graduating from medical school. Now married with two children, she'd settled nicely into a quiet suburban life but worried about the direction her little brother seemed to be heading.

She watched me over her shoulder as she poured herself a coffee.

"So what's this presentation about?" she asked.

"Privacy," I responded, checking my phone.

I'd given the talk a dozen times and had just published a best-selling book about it.

"You may want to go now if you wanna catch the train."

But I didn't care about punctuality that morning. I was riddled with angst, unable to reach Abby all night. I'd tracked her location to a hotel near her office before she'd turned off her phone and stopped responding to my texts. I hadn't slept a wink.

"Can't wait to divorce her," I told my sister.

"Rafie—"

"No. Marleigh. I know what you're going to say."

She walked over and pulled up a chair in the breakfast nook where I sat hunched, placing her arm around me just as she had when we were kids.

"Okay. I know this sucks, and you're right to be upset. And I'm not making excuses for Abby, but you can't do anything until you talk to her. Remember how Mom and Dad used to fight? Don't you remember those ultimatums and how insecure they made us feel?"

"What's your point?" I asked.

"That's not the way to do things. You have a kid."

"She was out all damn night, Mar! You don't understand. She's crazy!"

"Crazy like… Athena?"

I couldn't help but laugh. She'd heard the stories.

"It'll be okay," she tried to assure me.

"Really? What would you do if your husband stayed out all night?"

Marleigh took a sip from her mug and paused as if she were giving it serious thought.

"I'd fucking kill him," she said jokingly.

Two days later, I returned to a note on the bed from Abby. I dropped my bags as my heart sank, thinking she'd left me like Delilah.

> Rafie, we're in a tough spot. I don't want to keep fighting with you, but I don't know what you need from me, and you feel so far away. It's like there's somebody between us or something. Maybe we need some time apart? – Love, Ab

Torn between unresolved trust issues and a legitimate fear of abandonment, I stuck my head in the sand. I'd been through the mill with the adoption and was drained. I told my wife to forget about everything, and we tried to start fresh.

For the next several months, we pretended everything was okay.

But things weren't okay.

* * *

One afternoon, while running with Katie, she pulled me out of a crosswalk before I could be run over by a truck. My life passed before my eyes.

"Hey! Careful!" she said, saving me.

I took some deep breaths.

"You should have let it hit me. I'd have been better off," I jested.

She knew I was referring to my marriage. Smirking, she punched me in the shoulder and moved closer, but the light changed, and we kept running. Katie always seemed to be watching out for me, though, and I began trusting her more than my wife.

After the run, we returned to the studio gym. It was late on a Friday, and no films were released that weekend, so everyone was gone. Bathing areas were separate in the facility, but the sinks between the locker rooms were unisex. As I splashed my face, I saw her pass behind me in the mirror, wearing a white towel. She stopped for a moment, sensing my eyes were upon her. Seductively, she dropped the cloth and briefly turned to her side. I stared at her slender back, from head to heel, deliberating whether to follow her.

God knows what would have happened.

* * *

It was a tenuous time, and I resented my wife, blaming her for anything and everything that wasn't going my way. I saw an exit ramp in Katie and convinced myself that we had more in common than I did with Abby. She was my Camilla Bowles, and my wife was Princess Diana. Me?—I was Charles, the smug dupe too insecure to work on my marriage.

Until my wife's birthday party that October, Abby didn't even know what was budding between Katie and me, but I couldn't keep it hidden any longer. I was following in the adulterous footsteps of my birth father, and much like Christopher's dad, Michael, I couldn't live with the guilt of an affair. I planned to take what I thought was the decent route and make a clean break rather than cheat.

Our attraction was apparent at Abby's party. As she and her friends looked on from a corner table, I put my hand around Katie's waist at the bar. My wife was humiliated. She stormed out, and I chased her to the parking lot across the street. The time had come to confess that I was thinking of leaving. I could barely keep up with her as she sprinted to her car, bawling. As I reached for her wrist, she swung around and slapped me.

We stood there for a moment, and I felt raindrops. Abby clutched the pendant I'd given her when we first met, collected herself, and lowered her head.

"You know, Raf. I know what happened to you. And I know you didn't deserve it. But even though you're a *bastard*, your kids don't have to be."

"What?" I said, grabbing her tight.

"Damn it! Isn't it obvious?"

"No. What are you talking about?" I shouted as she placed my hand on her belly.

It dawned on me that she hadn't had a drink the whole night.

She was pregnant again.

I drove us home. After Abby went to bed, I sat on our couch in the living room, knowing I had to decide whether to save my marriage or start anew. Could we stay together for the children, like my parents? They'd reunited partly for us kids, but Abby and I were of a different generation. What good would family life be if we stayed together out of a sense of duty instead of love?

Wait. *Did I still love my wife?* Yes, but I wasn't sure if I *trusted* her. That was the problem. The mistrust wasn't entirely her fault, either. It was seeded in the great lie of my adoption. But even if I could learn to trust her, what about all the vitriol? All the lamentable things that had been said between us? It was hard to get past, yet Mom and Dad had taught me that marriage was full of peaks and valleys. Was it reasonable to think the animosity between Abby and me could be overcome? What about our sacred vow, "for better or for worse?"

I didn't know what to do.

My young son began to cry in his crib. He'd been kept up by the arguing and was frightened. As I held him in my arms that night, he reminded me so much of myself. But he wasn't just my son anymore. He would be a big brother in a few months.

Abby was pretending to sleep when I slid into bed. Beside her on the nightstand was a Bible, and on top of that, the pendant I'd given her. I lay down, feeling so distant from her and God, and did something I hadn't done in far too many years—I prayed.

* * *

Three days later, I asked Katie to lunch at the studio's dining room. They seated us on the patio, across from Walter's table. She was anxious, unsure why I'd invited her out after everything that had transpired. I could tell she loved me.

"Katie," I said, looking into her watering eyes.

She came closer, taking my hand, hoping I'd been thinking about her. *I had.*

"What is it, Raf?" she asked, preparing herself.

The room went silent as if an electric current had surged through the building and blown out the lights, just like when I learned I'd been adopted—and the answer came.

She looked at me for a few seconds after that, then took her hands off mine, pulled her chair from the table, and left the dining room in tears. All I could hear were her stilettos clicking away on the tile floor as she walked out of my life.

I caught a glimpse of Walter as he took a sip from his glass and wiped his lips with a napkin. As I sat alone, the dining room chatter returned as if the scene had never been shot. The room felt empty, though, like something else had vanished.

It was the monster.

I'd starved it to death.

Author's Note

F. Scott Fitzgerald earned a small fortune laying bare the intimate lives of the rich and famous in a series of novels and short stories written throughout a decadent era much like ours. Yet while his 1925 *The Great Gatsby* remains a staple of the American canon, critics have denigrated his narratives as devoid of the intellectualism that characterized less commercially successful literature of that time.

To the broader audience, however, the author's appeal has always been his astute observations of morality in motion. His subtle, melodic illustrations of complex, damaged individuals continue to resonate across all social strata. The material wealth of Fitzgerald's tragic characters is perhaps the least valuable thing about them. He believed life was about people and their relationships, not their money.

I do, too.

My goal in *The Bastard of Beverly Hills* was to strip the paint and varnish from portraits of people I've known, some for decades, and let their skeletons speak for themselves. No memoir can be free of bias, but I have no bridges to burn here. I've changed a few names in the book out of respect for private individuals and built composites from others. What's left of the record is as close to how it originally played when I first bought it—skips, scratches, and all.

Getting the rhythm of these vignettes to harmonize was a challenge. Although I came from a family of musicians, I didn't inherit their gifts. So I took inspiration for the story's cadence from tales I'd read as a boy and shaped the narrator's voice based on my father, Ray, who died shortly before publication. His full name was *Raymond Albert Moscatel,* like my brother and youngest son. The book is dedicated to each of them.

Structurally, this work is inspired by a traditional *Bildungsroman,* alluded to in the chapter *Quests.* It's segmented into seven chapters, an homage to Christopher Booker, whose 2004 *The Seven Basic Plots* encouraged me to draw them all together into one story arc. The character Nella is the mysterious widow mentioned in the introduction who initially suggests that literary approach.

Lastly, in writing *The Bastard,* I've described behavior and attitudes that don't reflect who I am now. But that doesn't prohibit me or anybody from committing to a life of forgiveness, charity, and love. It's been my aim since coming to terms with the good, bad, and ugly of my adoption. Like anybody, I'm a work in progress, but I'm no longer afraid of the monsters that haunted me from the dark recess of my youth.

Neither should you be.

Acknowledgment

Without Abby, my resilient, patient wife, closest friend, and editor, this book would never have made it out of my thick head. She scrutinized each draft while caring for our three wild and lovable children, Joel, Isabel, and Albert. Thank you, sweetheart, for helping bring *The Bastard* to life.

To my parents, Eleanor and Raymond, who provided me with the life I shared across these seven chapters, I thank you with every bone in my body. May you rest in peace, Dad.

I also owe a debt of gratitude to my sisters, especially Marleigh. Her love of literature helped nurture this book. She was the wind in my sails throughout the storms of my youth and never threw me overboard.

To Duncan Murrell for helping make the content of this book its *character*. He believed in its intrinsic value and promised me, "you'll know when it's done."

To the Landons and the memory of their parents, Michael & Lynn, with whom our family shared life, laughter, and friendship over many decades. This recollection would not be the same without those impermeable memories. And with the same love, I thank the Sterling, Barish, Hill, and Nash families, all of whom lost their sons like we lost Albert. I pray that sharing their stories may help other young people remember how loved they are.

And lastly, to almighty God, who saved me from the monster.

About the Author

RAFAEL MOSCATEL is the author of the best-selling business book series *Tomorrow's Jobs Today* and director of *The Little Girl with the Big Voice*, a critically acclaimed documentary. He lives in Northwest Montana with his wife, three feral children, and a poodle ill-equipped for the rigor of rocky mountain living. *The Bastard of Beverly Hills*, a memoir, is his third book.

You can connect with me on:

https://rafaelmoscatel.com

https://twitter.com/Rafael_Moscatel

https://www.facebook.com/authorrafaelmoscatel

Subscribe to my newsletter:

https://rafaelmoscatel.com/newsletter

CPSIA information can be obtained
at www.ICGtesting.com
Printed in the USA
LVHW040721260423
745312LV00008B/45/J